NEVER THE SAME

15
SMALL
GROUP
STUDIES
ON
KNOWING
GOD

JEFF KINLEY

David C. Cook Church Ministries—Resources
A division of Cook Communications Ministries
Colorado Springs, CO/Paris, Ontario

GREAT GROUPS
The Main Thing Series
Never the Same Leader's Guide
© 1994 David C. Cook Publishing Co.

All rights reserved. No part of this book may be reproduced in any form without the written permission of the publisher, unless otherwise stated in the text.

Unless otherwise noted, Scripture quotations are from the Holy Bible, New International Version (NIV), © 1973, 1978, 1984 by International Bible Society. Used by permission of Zondervan Bible Publishers.

David C. Cook Church Ministries—Resources
A division of Cook Communications Ministries
4050 Lee Vance View; Colorado Springs, CO 80918-7100
Cable address: DCCOOK
Edited by Mark Syswerda
Cover and interior design: Jeff Sharpton, PAZ Design Group
Cover illustration: Ken Cuffe
Printed in U.S.A.

ISBN: 0-7814-5109-4

ABLE OF Contents

Great Stuff about *Great Groups!*

Welcome to *Great Groups*—a new concept in youth ministry resources from David C. Cook.

Great Groups is a three-tiered series of studies created for high schoolers and young adults who are at various stages of spiritual development. The three tiers—designed to move young people from being casual about Christianity to becoming committed followers of Jesus Christ—look like this:

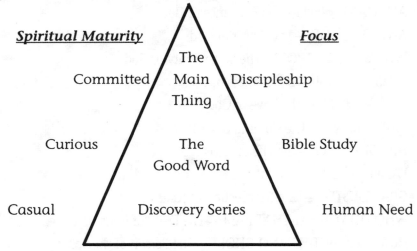

Great Groups was created because:

• Not all young people are at the same stage of spiritual development;

• Intentional ministry is needed to guide people toward greater spiritual commitment;

• Real life change is possible through studying the Bible individually and discussing it together in small groups;

• Many young people are ready to lead discussion groups, so these studies encourage peer leadership;

• No two small groups are the same, so these studies pay attention to group dynamics.

Discovery Series—entry-level studies for seekers and those who've grown up in the church, but who may not have a complete understanding of what it means to be a Christian. These studies help people discover who they are from God's perspective and how that can make a difference in every area of their lives. The *Discovery Series* assumes group members have little or no Bible background. Minimal advance preparation needed.

The Good Word—inductive studies for those who are curious about what the Bible really says. These studies help young people develop lifelong Bible study skills that will challenge them to feed themselves from Scripture. *The Good Word* series assumes group members have little or some Bible background. Moderate advance preparation needed.

The Main Thing—discipleship studies for those who want to be followers of Jesus Christ. These studies will challenge group members to take their faith seriously. *The Main Thing* series assumes group members have some or extensive Bible background. Thorough advance preparation needed.

FOREWORD

They're out there.

You know who I'm talking about. The people at church who are there only to see and be seen, instead of to learn about and worship the Lord Jesus Christ.

That's right—casual Christians.

And although you can find them in every youth group meeting room and every school hallway, you can also find passionate, committed Christians who are looking to grow closer to God.

This book, *Never the Same*, is a tool that can help teenagers do just that—grow closer to God.

But it's not a book designed just to help make Christians *feel* closer to God. This book is designed to help them *know* God better. It takes an indepth look at the attributes and characteristics of the Triune God, focusing on God the Father, God the Son, and God the Holy Spirit.

Too many folks trash American teenagers, and tell them that they aren't smart enough or disciplined enough to learn and live the heavy stuff. I just don't buy that.

That's why students can benefit from this book. It will challenge them, motivate them, and hopefully solidify their walk with God—a God who becomes closer and closer to them day by day.

So grab your shovels and dig into it. Your group can handle it, and everyone can grow from it.

Dawson McAllister

INTRODUCTION

Dear Friend,

Years ago, a friend of mine gave me the greatest challenge of all—to get to know God. I took that challenge, and my life was *never the same*.

I want this book to do the same for you and your group members! If you're fed up with "fast food" Bible lessons, and you've figured out there are no such things as "drive-through disciples" and "microwave ministries," then this book is for you.

It's a book for young people who want to know God—not just know about Him, but really know Him—personally, intimately, and deeply. In it, you and your group will explore what it means to be a disciple who experiences God as your Father, Jesus as your Savior, and the Holy Spirit as your Guide.

If, however, you're looking for the "magic curriculum," then keep looking.

Preparing these studies will take time, thought, and effort. It will require that you study them yourself if you want to impact your group members. But the reward is worth it. You will see changed lives that come from a face-to-face encounter with God.

And isn't that what you really want?

So take the challenge. Grab your Bible, a pen, and some friends and prepare yourselves to be *Never the Same!*

Jeff Kinley

How to Use This Bible Study

What Materials Will You Need?

To get started you will need a Bible (we used the New International Version), this leader's guide, a corresponding disciple's journal, a pencil or pen, and if you'd like, a notebook.

In order to lead the study properly, you will need to work through the questions in the disciple's journal along with familiarizing yourself with the information and questions in this leader's guide. Not all questions from the journal are reprinted in the leader's guide, so you will need both the journal and the guide.

Why a Small Group Bible Study?

Jesus believed in small group ministry. Though He spoke often to large crowds, the majority of Jesus' time and teaching was spent with just twelve men. To large crowds He spoke primarily about salvation. But to His small group, the topic was discipleship—how to know and follow Him.

The Bible says Jesus chose these men that "they might be with him" (Mark 3:14). This is the heart of small group ministry—time together sharing our lives and God's Word with one another. Jesus chose this approach to ministry because He knew it would make the greatest impact in their lives. And apparently it worked because you and I are the result of that impact on His small group. This is what Paul meant in his letter to young Timothy—"And the things you have heard me say in the presence of many witnesses entrust to reliable men who will also be qualified to teach others" (II Timothy 2:2).

So why a small group? Three reasons:

1. Intimacy—In a small group, you are free to be yourself, to get personal, and to grow close to one another.

2. Influence—In a small group, you can influence a few key people in a powerful way, and at the same time be held accountable by those whom you love.

3. Insight—In a small group, you not only learn from your own discoveries, but also from the insights of others.

Isn't that all we need?

What Kind of Bible Study Is This?

This is a Bible study series designed to "wear out" your Bible. In other words, it gets you into God's Word. It is you and your Bible, one-on-one. It is for you when you want to get everything you can out of the Bible. By the time you finish this book, your Bible should feel like a baseball glove at the end of the season—well worn and comfortable in your hand.

Your group members will get to know their Bibles better by looking up verses, cross-referencing, thinking about what they have read, and brainstorming ways to make God's truth real in their daily lives. As you come to different passages of Scripture, the disciple's journal asks questions that help your group members discover what Scripture says, what it means, and how to apply it. They will gain a greater knowledge of God's Word along with a deeper understanding of how to practically live it out. They will write in their journals and make notes in their Bibles as well—underlining, circling, highlighting. As they commit to this process, the Bible will come alive. They will begin reading God's Word in living color. The result—no more boring Bible studies.

But the greatest benefit of this kind of study is that, together, you will come face-to-face with God Himself. God speaks to us through His Word. And every time we study the Bible, we are spending time with Him. What could be more important than that? The outcome of this is that you grow closer to God and stronger in your faith. As you grow, your love for Christ will too, along with your motivation to serve Him.

Isn't that what we all want?

Who Leads the Bible Study?

Anyone in the group can lead, provided he or she is willing to do a little extra preparation beforehand. The good news is that you don't have to be a youth pastor, adult, Bible expert, or eloquent teacher. With the tips, suggestions, and insights found in this leader's guide, anyone can confidently lead this study. The leader's guide will not only help you understand the passages being studied, but will also give you the tools needed to help other group members discover the truth for themselves. Instead of coming across as a know-it-all, you will be more like a quarterback—a fellow teammate who points the way. This will enable you to make it easier for people in the group to share what they have learned during their private study time.

Don't be afraid if someone misses the point on a certain question or comes up with an off-the-wall comment. Instead of labeling the answer as "wrong," direct attention back to the verse. Let God's Word be the final authority. Don't allow the group to get sidetracked or argue. While some debate can be healthy, it is best to stick to the topic you are discussing.

The exciting thing about leading this way is that everyone gets the opportunity to discuss what they are learning. It requires them to think about what they have studied. It gives them the chance to bounce their thoughts off others and to grow from their friends' insights. It is fellowship at its best!

What Version of the Bible Should the Group Use?

The Scripture printed in the disciple's journal is the New International Version. This version is recommended for use in the group. For the most part, it is best when everyone is using the same version of the Bible. However, sometimes having another translation available helps to bring out the meaning of a verse more clearly. But the important thing is that each student have his or her own Bible.

The Format

The study for *Never the Same* (and each study in *The Main Thing* series) breaks down into three five-week units. Each of these units is an important part of each book, so it is best to study the book in its entirety. However, if you are limited because of time, you could focus on just one unit of five chapters.

You also need to decide as a group how long each study time will be. You should allow a minimum of forty minutes for the study itself, plus five to ten minutes of prayer.

Here is a suggested format of a meeting, plus some suggested times.

1 Getting Started (10-15 minutes)

One of the most important parts of your time together. You can use this time to welcome new people to the group, encourage people to mingle, and get into the frame of mind to discuss the study for the week.

Start on time. This shows you respect your group's commitment to be there. Take a few minutes at the beginning of your group time to catch up with each other. Discipleship must take place in the context of relationships. Ask group members how they are doing and what has been happening in their lives over the past week. Any special announcements could be given at this time as well. But though this is an important time, don't allow it to derail you from getting into the study. Keep it short.

Have a word of prayer before you launch into the study. This is essential because it gets the group into a mindset to learn and it lets everyone know you are dependent on the Lord to teach you.

To be specific, here is how the time is allotted:

Housekeeping (3-5 minutes)

This is the place for announcements (for example, a change in the meeting location or a schedule change) and other housekeeping tasks. Keep it short and sweet.

Icebreaking (5-10 minutes)

For the first few weeks, this section has lighthearted activities to enjoy. These activities will help people feel that the group is a safe place for sharing nonthreatening things. In later weeks, the activities become more serious and lead to deeper sharing.

Opening (5 minutes)

The group can choose to sing or not; however, some song titles are suggested. Do open in prayer. If you absolutely panic about leading in prayer, take advantage of the prayers and litanies we provide. It is not unspiritual to read a prayer—but truly pray it. Don't just rattle it off.

2 Bible Study (40-60 minutes)

A. Focus (Introduction, 3-5 minutes)

This short transition time allows you to use an activity or introductory questions found in the leader's guide. Give the group a brief overview of what you will be studying during your time together. Point out two or three things you will learn together as a result of that day's study. Whet their appetite by pointing out one or two practical benefits they will receive from studying the chapter.

B. Dig In (Observation and Interpretation, 30-40 minutes)

This is the very heart of your small group time. It is the time when each group member has a Bible and disciple's journal open in front of him or her. Expect each group member to have completed the Bible study beforehand. But in case someone forgot to prepare, the student can still contribute by looking up the verses with the rest of the group and taking part in the discussion. However, the more preparation, the better the discussion will be.

Your goal as the leader is to guide the group through the disciple's journal using the helps and suggestions found in the leader's guide. But most importantly, you want to make sure group members see the answers in their own Bible. You want them to leave with more than good notes in their journals. You want them to retain God's Word in their hearts. Feel free to add your own insights, illustrations, and practical suggestions, as well as looking at the interesting facts in the "Inside Insights" section. Encourage each person to take part in the discussion, sharing observations and insights. The way to do this is by simply asking the questions found in the disciple's journal. In this way, you are opening up the discussion to everyone.

At times, one or two eager students may tend to dominate a discussion. Since that can be intimidating to others in the group, direct some of your questions to particular individuals. Say something like, "David, what is this verse teaching us?" Also let each person read Scripture aloud. This is an easy way to draw people into the discussion. By doing this, you are making sure there are no "back row" Bible study members.

C. Reflect and Respond (Application, 5-10 minutes)

The goal of all Bible study is life change. Period. You want to produce more than just smarter Bible students. You want God to use this study to impact what they believe, how they think, and the way they live. And application is the key to this. After discovering what a passage says and after digging into it to find out what it means, you are ready to take what you have learned and make it real in your life. Here you want to brainstorm together on some concrete, practical ways to live out your faith. This is how you go from head knowledge to heart knowledge. You want to walk away knowing how your study changes your life. Sometimes the application will affect what they believe. Other times it will affect how they think. And many times, there will be something they need to do. A simple question to ask at the end of each study is, "How does this study change me?"

3 Sharing and Prayer (15-20 minutes)

Use this time to give each person the opportunity to relate prayer requests, praise God for answered prayer, and share personal concerns with the group. Begin by letting the group come up with at least one application out of your study you can pray for. Then take personal requests. Remember, if it is important to them, it is important to God.

But don't spend all of your time talking about prayer. Spend time actually praying together. Have open prayer, where anyone who feels led can pray out loud. Be creative with your prayer time. You could assign specific requests to certain students, let each person pray for the friend on the right or left, or focus on a particular topic, such as praise, thanksgiving, confession, etc. Be sure to use the prayer page at the end of each week so they can write down their requests and keep a record of God's faithfulness in answering those requests.

Finally, have a definite ending time each week and make sure you end on time. Respect your group members' schedules and don't forget to thank them for coming. If they want to hang around afterwards, that is fine. But be sure they know when the group time will officially be over.

The Disciple's Journal

It is recommended that you work your way through the appropriate session in the Disciple's journal as if you were one of the regular group members. This will help you get a feel for what group members will have learned before you supplement their study with information from the leader's guide.

To begin with, you will find that there is usually an intriguing activity or story to spark people's interest in completing the Bible study. Group members can have fun with it while making some exciting discoveries about their relationship with God.

Some, but not all, of the Scripture verses are printed in the journal. We try to print out the Scripture whenever there is a Scripture-marking activity—underlining, circling words, etc. However, we strongly encourage people to use their own Bibles as they work through these studies. We used the New International Version and you should too, if possible. But don't worry, use whatever translation you are most comfortable with.

There is space in the journal to write down responses to the questions. If more room is needed, write additional thoughts in some kind of notebook that will be easy to tote with you to the group Bible study. Make sure your notations are complete enough to make sense to you during the small group Bible study time. You may want to write down key words to spark your memory or you may need to write out complete thoughts—whichever works best for you.

There is also room to express oneself on the "Pray About It" page. Write out personal conversations with God. Talk to Him about, well, anything. Keep track of your requests and God's answers.

Encourage group members to always try to complete the entire week's study before the small group meeting, so that they can get the most out of other people's comments. This way, they won't miss out by trying to catch up on reading during the small group time.

Alive and Well!

The Existence of God

Overview

• to investigate several areas that help strengthen the validity of God's existence.

• to give group members confidence in both understanding and defending the existence of God.

Scripture: Romans 1:19, 20; II Timothy 3:16; II Peter 1:21; John 1:14, 18; Jeremiah 9:23, 24

1 Getting Started

One of the essentials for any small group meeting is—you guessed it—food. So you might have some chow ready. Chances are it will boost everyone's spirits and might create a more relaxed atmosphere for the group members to get to know each other better. Encourage them to introduce themselves to any group members they don't know.

Housekeeping

Hand out copies of the disciple's journal *Never the Same* to the group members. Encourage them to flip through and check it out. Meanwhile, explain some of the journal's features, making sure to mention the "Pray About It" section at the end of each week's session. Jokingly comment that you're not awarding a prize for the person with the cleanest, least worn, newest-looking journal at the end of the 15-week session. In other words, it's your job to encourage them to MARK IT UP!

That's what it's there for, whether it's underlining, circling, or just jotting down some thoughts.

Icebreaking

Pass out slips of paper to the group members. Explain that you want them to write down the name of the first member of the opposite sex they ever went out on a date with, and what they remember most about the date. Then collect the slips of paper in a hat, and have group members pick a slip out of the hat one at a time.

Have each group member read what's on his or her slip of paper and try to guess which group member that date is describing. Once group members have been identified, let them explain further about their "first date" (if willing).

Opening

If anyone plays the guitar among your group (or the piano if one is accessible to your meeting place), see if he or she would be willing to play music for weekly singing. Also, ask for a volunteer to help lead with the singing. (Although you don't *have* to have singing, it often can promote unity better than anything else.)

Regardless of the singing, here's a prayer that you may want to use or adapt as you begin the meeting time.

God, thank You for the opportunity we have to know You, as well as Your Son and Your Spirit. May we draw closer to You, our loving Father, as we try to understand You more and apply this understanding to the way we live our lives. In Jesus' name. Amen.

2 Bible Study

Focus

Thank all the group members for coming. Explain that you hope it will be a life-changing experience for all of you as you strive to know God—the Father, the Son, and the Holy Spirit—in a closer way that will change your lives.

Point out that today's meeting will start with the basics. Before anyone can get to know God better, one must be able to believe (and defend his or her belief) that God exists.

Have group members turn to page 11 in the journal and have them read the short story about Friedrich Nietzsche. Afterward, ask: **Why does it say Nietzsche denied God's existence?** (Because of all the evil in the world.)

Since most group members probably already believe in the existence of God, brainstorm together for a few minutes on question one of Section I to see how many reasons you can come up with why people might not believe there is a God. Then, let group members take a look at question two in Section I. Have them read the question and list four reasons God might give (if He was on trial) *for* His existence (have everyone do this without looking ahead in the journal!).

Have group members share their reasons together and compile a group list. "Dig in" to what the Bible has to say about the reasoning for God's existence.

Leader's Tip: *The other group members need to feel like you're just "one of them," but just the one who has taken the responsibility to guide the group. Show this by sharing personal experiences from your own life, admitting that you struggle with being close to God, etc. By seeing that you're not on an "ego trip" as the leader, the other group members will give you their respect and attention much quicker.*

Dig In

Ask any group member what he or she thinks is one of the "first" reasons God would give for His existence. (If no one mentions it, ask one of them what Genesis 1:1 says.)

Have group members answer question one in Section II. Ask: What, in your opinion, are some of the most powerful displays of God's act of creation (i.e., Grand Canyon, Rocky Mountains, etc.)?

INSIDE INSIGHTS

■ Though John 1:18 states that "No one has ever seen God . . .", sometimes in the Old Testament people were said to have seen God. (In Exodus 24:9-11, Moses, Aaron, Nadab, Abihu, and 70 elders of Israel saw the Lord.) But we are also told in the Old Testament that no one can see God and live (Exodus 33:20, where God is speaking to Moses). Therefore, those who saw God saw an appearance which God took on temporarily for that occasion. Apparently, they did not view God in His essential nature (refer again to Exodus 33:20 for proof).

■ The awesomeness of God isn't limited just to His *sight*, based on the fact that no one can see God and live (Exodus 33:20). God's *voice* also proves the awesome power of His existence. Psalm 29 describes the voice of the Lord as something that "thunders over the mighty waters," "is powerful . . . majestic," "breaks the cedars," "strikes with flashes of lightning," "shakes the desert," and "twists the oaks."

Ask someone to read Romans 1:20 and have everyone answer questions two and three in Section II. Afterward, ask: **When we read that people are without excuse when they don't believe in God, do you think it means people who have never even heard about God will be held accountable anyway?** Then read the mind-boggling tidbit of Sir Fred Hoyle, a noted British astronomer, on page 14 of the journal to put into perspective the overwhelming fact that the world has a Creator.

Explain that just as evidence that God exists is found by looking at creation, the external world, it is equally just as important to look *internally* for evidence of God's existence—that is, at our conscience.

Have group members go around the circle and, in 10 seconds, come up with a definition for what each of them thinks conscience means. After everyone's said his or her definition, state that it's something inside us that tells us what's right from wrong. Or, as one little boy put it, "The part of you that makes you tell your mother what you did wrong, before your sister does."

Ask someone to read Romans 1:19, and ask: **How do you think a conscience can show that God exists?**

Allow people to respond. You may want to point out that this claim is supported by the fact that every people and culture—from the most advanced to the most primitive—have basic moral values. Romans 1:19 states that a person has an inborn knowledge that a Supreme Being exists. Read Romans 2:15, and point out that people's consciences also bear witness that there is a God.

Explain that another reason God might give to support His existence would be common sense. Give the following example, and then ask group members if they can relate it to God's existence.

Jeff comes home for supper every night, and takes his place at the table where meat, potatoes, vegetables, bread, and other food sit waiting for him. But how did it get there? Could it just have magically appeared?

Explain that obviously the food was prepared, probably by someone. Tell group members that this is the cause-and-effect argument for God's existence. Explain that this argument states that every effect has a cause.

Just like Jeff's dinner was the effect, so it was caused by someone preparing it. Similarly, just as the universe or creation is an effect, it had to be caused by something or someone (God the Creator).

Challenge your group members to come up with an example along the lines of "Jeff and his dinner" that will make the same point that every effect has a cause. Then have group members share their examples together.

Explain to your group members that the next reason God would give in defending His existence would be the credibility of the Bible.

Recruit a group member to read II Timothy 3:16 and II Peter 1:21 and have people answer question one in Section V. Then ask them: **How would you respond to someone who argued that you can't use the Bible—God's own writings—to defend His existence because that would be biased?**

Let people respond, but be prepared to explain that if the Bible can be trusted as a credible document, then it can be used to defend God's existence. And tell them that you're going to look at proof that it is credible—prophetically, historically, and scientifically.

Give group members a few minutes to read through exhibits D, E, and F in Section V. Ask group members to share any other prophecies or historical things they can think of that have accurately taken place.

Ask your group members: **How do you think Jesus could help prove the existence of God?** Let anyone answer.

Have group members read John 1:14 and answer question one in Section VI. Also, have group members refer to John 1:18 along with 1:14 to help answer question 3. (Though God has never been seen in His essential being, Jesus Christ, through His existence on earth, has made God's glory known.)

Reflect and Respond

Up until now, you have been working through various methods of proving the existence of God. But now is a perfect time to ask three questions based on the assumption that God does exist. They are: "If there is a God, what is He like?" "Can He be known?" and "Am I accountable to Him?"

Have a group member read the story about the missionary on page 21 in the journal. When finished, mention that God can be known, by entering into a relationship through believing in Him.

If your group members are already Christians, have them answer questions seven and eight in Section VI of the journal.

Then ask group members: **Have you made understanding and knowing God the "ultimate goal" in your life? Or, like Jeremiah 9:23 states, has your life's aim been your own wisdom, or your own strength, or riches?**

Finally, ask: **If God called *you* to the "witness stand" to give testimony concerning His existence in your life, what would you say?** Give each person a chance to say a few words, and give them a minute or two to write down any responses in their journals.

3 Sharing and Prayer

Encourage group members to praise God for life's blessings when they pray, instead of just bombarding God with requests. Let group members know that your meeting time is an "open forum" for any request—love life, job, school, family, friends, career paths, or whatever is on their minds.

Also encourage group members to keep a written tab on other people's prayer requests and answered prayers in the back of their journals, enabling them to actually see how God answers prayer.

Close with a time of prayer, where you open it up for everyone to pray out loud who wants to. You (the leader) should close this week, but ask for volunteers in the coming weeks to close out the meeting in prayer.

Before group members leave, encourage them to complete Week Two in time for your next meeting.

WEEK 2 Awesome God!

The Power of God

Overview

• to let group members take a fresh look at God's power through various instances in the Bible.

• to help group members understand this available power and experience it in their own lives.

Scripture: selected passages depicting instances of God's power throughout history and in people's lives today

1 Getting Started

Housekeeping

Make any opening announcements that are needed, and welcome any new people to the group. Let them introduce themselves, if you think it's needed. Pass out copies of disciple journals to each of the new group members, but before you give the new people their journals, make them stand up and confess to the rest of the group what they wear when they go to bed each night (just a little something to lighten the mood!). Thank everyone for coming.

Icebreaking

Bring a one-pound bag of M&M's to the meeting. Pass around the bag and encourage each of your group members to take some. But also instruct them not to eat any until the bag makes its way back to you (although probably empty!). When all the group members have grabbed their fair share, explain that they all must say one thing that describes them (hobbies, most favorite things, least favorite, etc.) for *each* M&M that they took (This should draw a few laughs if anyone grabbed a whole handful!). This informal, getting-to-know time should help draw your group together before heading into the meeting time.

Opening

Since you and the rest of the group members are probably now on a "sugar high," you'll probably be in the mood for some upbeat praise choruses (which is doubly fitting, since this week's lesson is an upbeat topic!). Select some group favorites, but one suggestion you might sing is "Awesome God." Here's a prayer for you to either use or supplement with your own prayer.

Lord God Almighty, it is a privilege for us to worship You, and we humble ourselves before You. We also want to praise You for the power You have shown glimpses of in the Bible and throughout history, and we pray for a small portion of that same power in our own lives. In Jesus' name. Amen.

2 Bible Study

Focus

Let's assume that all group members have completed their journals before the meeting and aren't furiously scribbling in the pages at this very moment. Let group members describe one of the powerful things they've seen that they checked off in the list on page 24 of Section I in the journal. Be prepared to share one of your experiences as well.

After listening to some of the explanations, ask to see how many people checked off having seen God's power on the list. If any did, ask a few of them to explain. For those who didn't check it, tell them to think about why they didn't.

After some discussion, say that hopefully, this week's study will answer the three questions listed in the journal on page 24, Section I. Let people take a few moments to read over those questions before proceeding into the lesson.

Dig In

INSIDE INSIGHTS

■ There may be more to the Israelites' crossing of the Red Sea than meets the eye. The body of water that the NIV Study Bible traditionally calls the Red Sea is called *yam suph* in the Hebrew, which actually is the Sea of Reeds. In the Old Testament, this term, *yam suph*, does not necessarily cover the Red Sea, but perhaps the Bitter Lakes region, including Lake Menzaleh, which is in northern Egypt. Some claim the phrase *yam suph* could not refer to the Red Sea because reeds do not grow in salt water (of which the Red Sea is). Hence, the Israelites' crossing probably occurred at the southern end of Lake Menzaleh, not the Red Sea.

■ More on the Red Sea situation. Studies have shown that the reedy waters of the Bitter Lakes and Lake Menzaleh are able to be affected by strong east winds in a similar way as described in Exodus 14:21, ". . . the Lord drove the sea back with a strong east wind and turned it into dry land. The waters were divided. . . ." A somewhat similar "crossing of the Red Sea" was also reported to have been experienced, albeit on a small scale, by Aly Shafei Bey in 1945-46 (*Bulletin de la Societe Royale de Geographie d'Egypte*, XXI, August 1946, 231 ff.). Though in the biblical account, a miracle was obviously involved.

Recruit three volunteers to read the three passages listed under question one of Section II on page 25 of the journal. After the verses have been read, ask for three volunteers to explain what they answered.

Ask: How does it make you feel to read statements about the Lord like, "Is anything too hard for the Lord?" (Genesis 18:14) and "I know that you [God] can do all things" (Job 42:2)?

Discuss question two in Section II by having several group members read their definitions of the power of God. Then work together to come up with one group definition of God's power, drawing from everyone's individual definitions.

Tell all the group members to refer to the examples each of them came up with for question three of Section II. But instruct them not to mention any of them out loud. Instead, have group members gather in a circle to play this game.

Designate one person to start. He or she has five seconds to name an event from the Bible describing God's power. When he or she says one, then the person to the right must say one—in five seconds, then the next person to the right, then the next . . . and so on. If a group member can't think of one to say in the five seconds, or repeats one, that person is out. The last person left in the circle is the winner.

In essence, this is an exercise in recalling as many of these descriptions of God's power recorded in the Bible. A few examples might be: more known—parting of the Red Sea, feeding of the 5,000, etc.; less known—Elijah *running* ahead of Ahab who was *riding* in his chariot from Mt. Carmel all the way to Jezreel, a distance of around 20 miles.

Recruit three volunteers to read the three passages under question four on page 26, Section II. Let individuals go around the room one at a time and read off the movie titles they came up with for the three events.

After people have had a chance to say their titles, have the entire group "review" all the movie titles and vote on a favorite for each biblical event. Award small prizes to the people who came up with the winning titles.

Go around the room one at a time, and let group members answer question five in Section II.

Leader's Tip: *You may have noticed that some of your group members aren't the kind to just speak up in front of the others. Instances like getting group members to describe what they checked off on their power list in Section I and question five in Section II are great opportunities to get those quiet people to speak up, because they're not right-or-wrong answers. Just be sure to encourage them and thank them for sharing.*

You might want to be the first to respond to question seven in Section II of the journal. Then let other group members respond with their thoughts.

7. You read about the Israelites' reaction to one of God's displays of power (Exodus 14, 15). How do you think you would respond to such awesome examples of God's power?

After responses, say: **People today often hear about these displays of God's power, yet often write them off as nothing more than a good story. They can't fathom what really happened. To bring it closer to home, listen to this modern-day version:**

For some unknown reason, the entire population of your state is being chased after by the entire population of the state to the west of you (unless, of course, you live in California, Oregon, Washington, Alaska, or Hawaii). All of the people of that state—who aren't happy—pursue you until you come to the biggest body of water around where you live (which could be Pacific Ocean, Atlantic Ocean, Gulf of Mexico, one of the Great Lakes, the Mississippi River, etc.). You're trapped; but suddenly, before your eyes, the water divides and you walk safely over to the other side (wherever that is).

Take a few minutes to discuss question eight of Section II, but don't spend too much time as this topic of discussion could very well spill over into next week's meeting time.

 Work through Section III by letting group members share some of the key words from the passages listed in Section III. In case people have any difficulty, here are some helpful reminders for the verses:

Power to stand up for Christ (Romans 1:16); power to overcome temptation (I Corinthians 10:13); power to protect us from being separated from Him (John 10:28, 29); power to overcome problems (Isaiah 40:28-31); power to sufficiently meet our needs and more (Ephesians 3:20, 21).

All of God's power is best wrapped up in the last passage, Ephesians 3:20, 21, which says that God can do ". . . immeasurably more than all we ask. . . ." In other words, it's like your mom asking you to go to the supermarket to buy a loaf of bread, then giving you a $100 bill to buy it. It's like you wanting just 10 more minutes of sleep before getting up for school, and then finding out school's been cancelled because of snow. It's more than enough! (Although for some sleepyheads, no amount of sleep is ever enough!)

Here's a fun exercise that still emphasizes the idea of God's power being more than all we need for our lives. Have each group member try to think of a metaphor—similar to the two above—that characterizes how God has the power to do more than we could ever ask. Let people share their "creations" with the rest of the group.

Reflect and Respond

Ask: **Now that we're familiar with God's power, both throughout history and what it can do in our own lives, how can we "grab ahold" of that power?**

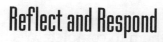

Spend a few minutes discussing the two principles given in the "Keep In Mind" section on page 29 of the journal. Have your group members brainstorm together to come up with several other ways to put oneself in a position to experience God's power in addition to the list already provided.

Here are a few other questions that could be added to your discussion.

• **Have you been in any of the "positions" that were listed in the journal or that were thought of in the brainstorming session? If so, did you experience God's power? Explain.**

• **What might be some positions you would like to see yourself personally involved with where you would be able to experience God's power?**

Focus on the second principle by sharing (you may want to do this first) any time(s) in your life where you tried to rely on your own strength instead of God's, and you failed. Ask if any group members are willing to share some of their own experiences.

3 Sharing and Prayer

Close your meeting with a time of prayer. First, however, encourage your group members to write in their journals one request they would have for God concerning His power in their lives. Encourage those who are willing to share with the group what their request was to do so.

Go around the room one at a time and have people pray out loud, if desired. Designate someone to close in prayer. Thank God for taking on our burdens in life and that we don't have to rely simply on our own strength and power. Instead, we have His to lean on—but He wants us to ask Him for it. Pray that people would never be guilty of putting God in a box, but would ask God to freely pour out His power and blessings in our lives.

Before group members leave, encourage them to complete Week Three in time for your next meeting.

WEEK 3 Who's in Control?

The Sovereignty of God

Overview

• to show group members, through the Bible, that God has everything in their lives under control and in His care.

• to build up group members' faith to the point of trusting Him completely with their lives.

Scripture: Psalms 45:6; 115:3; 135:6; Daniel 4:35; Isaiah 40:21-24; Romans 8:28

1 Getting Started

Housekeeping

You might want to bring in a few extra Bibles for any group members who forgot to bring theirs to the meeting. But mostly, this is a good time for you to look for a little feedback from group members on how they're doing with their journals. Ask questions regarding whether or not they're enjoying it, the amount of time it's taking them per weekly session, when during the day they're completing it, etc.

Icebreaking

Bring a small rubber ball (the super bouncy kind) to the meeting. Have group members get chairs and sit in a circle. One group member needs to stand in the middle of the circle. One person sitting in the circle will have "control" (a convenient little name for the ball!). NOTE: *However, the person in the middle is* not *to know who has the ball to start.* When signaled, the people in the circle will begin passing the ball from left to right around the circle in the following manner:

All group members will clasp hands with the group member both to their left and to their right. Then, in a steady rhythm, group members will bring their hands together to give the impression that they are *all* transferring the ball from their left hand to their right. Keeping rhythm, they will then spread their clenched hands back out until they clasp hands again, giving the impression that they are *all* passing the ball to the person on their right.

The natural procession will be "hands apart, hands together, hands apart, hands together," as the ball is passed (hopefully, it's done conspicuously) around the room. The idea is that the person standing in the middle doesn't know who actually has the ball, but is trying to determine who does by watching closely.

When you (the leader) say "Stop," all group members in the circle must hold their clenched hands out in front of them. The person in the middle must then make a guess as to who he or she thinks has the ball. Give all the group members a shot at standing in the middle and guessing who has "control" (i.e., the ball).

When the activity's finished (and everyone's tired of "hands apart, hands together"), ask: **How did you feel when you were in the middle and had to figure out who actually had "control"? What things did you look for when you were trying to figure it out?** After some response, ask: **When have there been some times where you wondered who, or what, had "control" of your life, where you felt like it was spinning *out* of control?**

Let anyone share who is willing; then say: **We probably all feel sometimes like life is a little bit out of control. But today's study will hopefully let us realize and be confident that God is in control, and is watching over the lives of each of us.**

Opening

One song that might be appropriate for your group to sing is "Control" by Janet Jackson (just kidding!). Seriously, think of some songs that praise God for His control of our lives. One that is probably familiar to everyone is "Trust and Obey," by John Sammis. If you're feeling a little bit rowdy, a song you might use is the childhood classic, "He's Got the Whole World in His Hands," complete with the different verses and actions.

In your opening prayer, focus on praising God for the security we have in knowing that He is watching over us and has everything in our lives under control.

2 Bible Study

Focus

Have one of your students read the opening story of Week 3 on page 31 in the journal. After the story has been read, ask group members if any of them have had similar experiences, either on a horse or during some other activity.

Once finished, refer to the author's statement about a poll that said 65 percent of Americans think the world is out of control. Ask: **If that pollster would have asked you whether or not you thought the world was out of control, how would you have answered? Explain.**

Before digging into the session, tell group members to close their journals. Pass out small slips of paper to each of them. Say: **Before we try to figure out what all this stuff about the sovereignty of God means, let's see if we know how sovereignty is spelled.**

Instruct them to—without looking in their journals—attempt to spell the word "sovereignty" on the slip of paper and to then sign their name. When finished, have them pass the slips of paper to you. Go through and check everyone's spellings, awarding a small prize to whoever spelled it right.

You may also want to award a prize to the person whose spelling attempt was the worst, based on a group vote. This may lighten the mood and help make the weaker spellers feel less uncomfortable.

INSIDE
INSIGHTS

■ Reuben, Joseph's oldest brother, had convinced the other brothers not to kill Joseph but to throw him into an old, empty well instead. Then, in Genesis 37:25-28 we read that a group of foreign merchants came by so Joseph's brothers sold Joseph as a slave to the merchants. But in vss. 29, 30, we read that Reuben thought Joseph was still in the well, only to be surprised that he wasn't there. The question is: **Where was Reuben when the brothers sold Joseph to the merchants?** In those days, foreigners (especially foreign merchants) could not be trusted not to steal a few prime animals. So Reuben, the most conscientious brother (exemplified by his sparing of Joseph's life in vss. 21, 22), was in all likelihood out guarding the sheep until the foreigners had passed on. When Reuben would have returned to the other brothers, Joseph would have been sold and gone by that time.

■ God's sovereignty not only saved Joseph's life throughout his whole ordeal, but saved perhaps the lives of the entire known world at that point. The lives of the Israelites, the Egyptians and all the other nations that bought food from Egypt during the seven years of famine, were also saved due to God's sovereignty.

Dig In

Recruit three volunteers to read the three passages in question one of Section I on page 32 of the journal. Ask for other volunteers to mention what these verses say about God's sovereignty.

After some discussion, say: **Obviously, God can do "whatever pleases Him." But if God does whatever pleases Him, how do you respond to someone whose life is full of experiences that aren't very pleasing?**

This is a tough issue for young people to wrestle with, but explain that it's dangerous to get one's view of what God is like based on *experience.* If that's the case, God may be kind and loving to one person, but cruel and unloving to another—depending on their life experiences.

Let's look in the Bible to find out a little more about God and this sovereignty business of His.

First, have group members turn to page 33 in their journals, and recruit someone to read the opening illustration in Section II. Then discuss how group members answered question one in Section II.

1. But what does the Bible say about God's rule and His ability to control His universe?

- Psalm 45:6

- Isaiah 40:21-24

Wow, the passage in Isaiah likens us to grasshoppers when we are compared to God. But often times, we seem to think *we* are God, and that we can control everything in our lives ourselves. What are some indicators in today's society that would cause us to believe that human beings think they are in control and that they have made their rights more important than anything?

See what group members come up with for answers. A few things you might mention to the group as answers might include:

- We live in a democratic society where *we* choose our leaders.

- We've "kicked" God out of public life (i.e., prayer), so all that's left is *our* desires and wishes.

- Personal, individual choice has become society's "god."

- Any form of "religion" is personal, strictly between you and God.

Read the cruise ship example on page 34 under question three in Section II. Then ask group members how they answered question four, and to share any other analogies they came up with.

Here's a simple activity that can make the same point that God is still in control and can accomplish His purposes without controlling all humanity like puppets.

Have everyone stand at one end of your meeting place. Explain that you want each of them, one at a time, to proceed to the other end of the meeting place, touch the wall (or if you're outside, designate a certain tree or something), and come back to the starting point. The only catch is that each person must go down and back in a totally different manner than everyone else.

For example, one person may simply walk, another may skip, another may hop, another may walk backwards, another may somersault all the way down and back, etc. Encourage group members to be creative.

When everyone's finished, point out how the main purpose—traveling down and back—was still accomplished, without controlling everyone's actions. In other words, there are certain aspects of freedom in God's sovereignty.

Get some group members to read the passages related to Joseph and Jesus in Section III. Then ask group members for their responses to the questions regarding Joseph and Jesus under Section III.

 What happened to Joseph that may have caused him to question God's sovereignty? According to Genesis 50:20, what perspective did Joseph gain concerning God's sovereignty in his life? What does Acts 2:23 say about God's sovereignty in the death of Christ? In what way did God plan this tragedy for good?

Reflect and Respond

Ask: **When has there been a time in your life where you may have felt like Joseph or like Jesus—rejected, forgotten by God, etc.?** Spend some time in discussion, then read Romans 8:28 aloud.

Say: **Knowing what Romans 8:28 says, explain how you responded to that tough situation in your life. Do you think God was working in that situation for good, or do you have a hard time accepting the promise that Romans 8:28 makes? Explain.**

Leader's Tip: You may want to mention that it's okay to struggle with thinking that Romans 8:28 (or other similar promises, like Ephesians 1:11) will be the instant cure-all for the hurt and pain that life's problems can cause. Emphasize that life's problems—especially when they hit close to home—aren't soothed over by mindlessly quoting one of the Bible's promises. It is only when we really trust *in what God's Word says about His sovereignty that we can truly handle our tough times.*

Read the following list of "less than desirable" situations to your group members. Have them write down the three situations they would hate to be in the most and have them number them one through three. Then have them finish the following sentences for each situation:

Knowing me in situation #___ , I would tend to:

But knowing God is in control in situation #___ , I would want to:

"LESS THAN DESIRABLE" SITUATIONS

- you cause your team to lose the championship game
- a close friendship goes sour
- your parents decide at the last minute not to let you go on the youth winter retreat ski trip
- your family decides to move
- your boyfriend/girlfriend's family decides to move
- you come home from school to find out your house has been robbed and all your valuables are gone
- your grades aren't exactly going up
- your parents make you get a job and you hate it
- your doctor discovers a mysterious "lump" during a routine examination
- a semi-close friend at school takes his/her own life

3 Sharing and Prayer

Spend some time letting group members share what situations were their least desirable ones, and how they could see themselves responding both with and without God's help. Encourage this to be an informal time so that group members can be comfortable, open, and honest about how think they would react in those situations.

Close with a group time of prayer, letting anyone pray who wants to pray. Thank God for letting us see in the Bible how, despite having not-so-great circumstances, He is still in control and just wants us to trust solely and fully in Him.

Before group members leave, encourage them to complete Week Four in time for your next meeting.

WEEK 4 Holy Smokes!

The Holiness of God

Overview

• to expose group members, through the Bible, to the awesome holiness of God.

• to help group members take steps for God's holiness to permeate and purify their lives.

Scripture: Isaiah 6:1-7; 55:8, 9; 57:15; I John 1:5; I Peter 1:15, 16

1 Getting Started

Housekeeping

Whereas last week you received feedback regarding how the journals were going, this week is a good time to get group members' impressions of the group meeting time itself. Ask them what they like, dislike, or would change about the group as well as if the group time has been beneficial.

Make note of people's comments and/or suggestions to change the meeting time a little bit (such as when, where, how, etc.), and try to incorporate these changes into the meeting time in the next few weeks.

Icebreaking

When all the group members get quiet (it could take a while), begin speaking these words: **Having a job interview, that first** "talk" with your girlfriend's father, taking the ACT or SAT, playing against the top-ranked team in the state, being challenged by your teacher to defend your beliefs in class, meeting your favorite actor/actress, wearing a brand new swimsuit at the local pool, witnessing to someone at school, being pulled over by a police officer, performing at a musical recital—what do all these things have in common? Before group members can blurt out what they think, say: I'll tell you—The "I" word. That's right. Intimidation. Who doesn't start to sweat or get all clammy in these types of situations? Okay, so maybe some aren't as intimidating as others, but there's probably something on that list that doesn't sound too comforting.

Explain to group members that you want them to write down three things or situations that intimidate them the most. Give group members a few minutes to come up with their lists. Then go around the group, one at a time, and let people explain what they wrote on their lists, if they're willing.

Leader's Tip: In this type of activity where some personal, vulnerable information might be made public, you may want to be the first one to share. This shows your willingness to let everyone know that you have fears. By being open, it will create an atmosphere of acceptance that will encourage other group members to be honest and sincere as well.

When everyone's finished, ask if anyone wrote on his or her list: "God's holiness." Explain that during this study time you're going to take a look at God's holiness, and how it is something that should be intimidating to everyone. Explain that you'll also see our inadequacy when compared to God's holiness, as well as some steps to take to try to emulate God's holiness in our own lives.

Opening

This week's lesson is on a more serious note, so you may want to sing some more meaningful songs. One suggested song is the classic hymn "Holy, Holy, Holy, Lord God Almighty!" by Reginald Heber. This song should be sung reverently to the Lord, and is especially moving when sung a cappella. You could even let this reverent singing to the Lord serve as your group's prayer time, if desired.

2 Bible Study

Focus

Recruit a volunteer to read the opening story, "But He's Bigger and Better Than Me" on page 39 of the journal.

After the story's been read, say: **Even though most of us will never have to deal with the intimidation of facing James Worthy on the basketball court, there is someone—or something—that towers over us even more. That someone is God, and that something is His holiness.**

But God's holiness can also be a great comfort to us if we see it in the right context. Let's see how.

Ask group members how they rated both God's holiness and their own holiness in question one, Section I.

The first point you want to get across to everyone is that God is different from us, and that basically, that's what holiness means. Point out that sometimes people get the idea that God isn't that different from us, and that they've kind of got Him figured out that way. So rather than being a God whom they reverently fear, God becomes a good "pal" instead.

Let's read in the Bible where it indicates that there is quite a gap or gulf between humans and God.

Dig In

Get two group members to read Isaiah 57:15 and Isaiah 55:8, 9 starting with page 42 of Section II.

When the other volunteer has finished reading Isaiah 57:15, say: **Based on** this verse, humanity is "lowly" and God is "high and lofty."

After the volunteer has read Isaiah 55:8, 9, ask: **Based on these verses, how would rate people and God? What do you think the word "higher" means in this passage?**

(Section II) 1. What do you think it means when Scripture says that God is "high and lofty"? Let group members respond and then have someone read Isaiah 6:1-7. As a group, go over the answers you came up with for questions five and six in Section II.

We've been looking at God's holiness, comparing it to our lack of holiness. Now let's look at the angelic creatures mentioned in Isaiah 6 that were around God and His holiness.

(Section III) 1. Why do you think that the seraphim covered their faces and feet in God's presence?

Let people offer responses. The fact that they could not bear to look at God or stand in His presence is apparently the reason.

In I John 1:5, John describes God as "light," and that "in Him there is

INSIDE
INSIGHTS

■ Isaiah chapter 6 is the *only* place in the Bible to mention the seraphim, the six-winged angelic beings that were leaders of divine worship to God on His throne in heaven.

■ The Hebrew root word for seraphim is *sarap,* meaning "to consume with fire." This gives the seraphim a purifying ministry through fire, which would coincide with Isaiah 6:6, 7, where one of the seraphs placed a live coal on Isaiah's lips, cleansing Isaiah's sin.

no darkness." How might you describe people like you and I in terms of light and darkness?

Discuss together the reactions of other men in the Bible (question one, Section IV) on page 44 of the journal. Then discuss question two of Section IV, which asks your group members how they think they would have reacted if they were those men in the Bible.

Reflect and Respond

As a group, answer question four in Section IV. Let any group members share who are willing.

Go around the group one person at a time, and ask group members what area of life they selected as being the toughest to live as if God was right there with them. Encourage them to explain why, if they're willing. For example, maybe when someone gets angry, they tend to use profanity without even thinking about it.

Here's an idea to help remind your group members that God and His holiness are present in every area of their lives. Everywhere they go, have them picture God sitting somewhere close by.

Then close by saying: **God's holiness can make us holy because it motivates us to ask for and receive His forgiveness and cleansing. With His strength, Christians should strive to be holy like God, because we are commanded in I Peter 1:15, 16, ". . . so be holy in all you do; for it is written: 'Be holy, because I am holy.' "**

3 Sharing and Prayer

Use this time to give group members a chance to "air out" any fears of feelings regarding the "convicting" area of God's holiness.

Explain that Christians who are seeking to please God have no reason to feel guilty or ashamed. Point out that when people experience salvation in Christ, they receive God's complete forgiveness and are made holy (Hebrews 10:10). That experience can be called their "positional holiness," that is, the fact that they are children of God. But stress that this week's study has been talking about "practical holiness," that is, the lifestyle of living pure, clean lives everyday, in everything we do.

Close by praying in reverence to the Most Holy God, requesting for the strength to follow the command of I Peter 1:16, which states to "Be holy, because I [God] am holy."

Before group members leave, encourage them to complete Week Five in time for your next meeting.

WEEK 5 Safe at Home

The Love of God

Overview

• to help group members see what God's love is and how He loves them.
• to help group members to experience God's love first-hand.

Scripture: selected verses that define and describe God's love for us

1 Getting Started

Housekeeping

This meeting marks the end of a journey—sort of. Actually, you'll be finished with the first unit in this book, which brings your group to a "fork in the road." Decide amongst yourselves if you want to keep plowing ahead or if you want a brief, one-week hiatus. If you've decided to take a week off, make a mental note to *remind* people to fill in their journals for the meeting in two weeks (because two weeks can make a lot of people forgetful!).

After you've reminded them, remind them again. Then, you might want to award a small prize for whoever has the most "marked-up journal," to motivate everyone to be underlining, highlighting, circling, jotting (or just plain doodling!).

Icebreaking

Divide group members into groups of three people each. Tell them that since this week's meeting is about the love of God, you're going to have a little contest. Explain that when you say, "Go," each team will have three minutes to think of and write down as many songs as possible with the word "love" in the title.

Once the three minutes are up, have a person from each group read that group's list of songs, until every group has had it's list read.

Here's how the scoring should go: Award each group one point for every song on its list. Also, award each group two points for every song on its list that no other group thought of! That should motivate the group members to put on their thinking caps!

If a group has a song that is "questioned" by other groups, that group must be able to sing enough of it to prove that it is, in fact, a legitimate song. The group with the most points is the winner.

Award winning group members a small "love" prize, such as a rose or some heart-shaped candy.

Then say: **There's a lot of talk about love these days. We are a culture obsessed with the idea of love. You see love on television, love at the movies, love in the magazines, love at school, love on the radio, love practically everywhere. But is it "real love"? Exactly what is "real love"? Most importantly, what does it *really* mean to say that "God loves you"?**

That's exactly what we hope to learn from this week's study.

 ## Opening

There may be some songs about the love of God that you may want to sing. One song you might use is the praise song "O, How He Loves You and Me." But if you feel all "song-ed out" after the Icebreaking activity, another option you might try is to let group members browse through their Bibles and pick out some of their favorite verses about love to read to the rest of the group.

In your prayer, thank God for His ultimate love for us He showed by sending His own Son to die on our behalf. Ask that your lives would be an example of His love as you try to show that love to a needy world.

2 Bible Study

Focus

Read the opening story about King Frederick's "language experiment" on page 47 of the journal. Get your group members' feelings about the story.

Then ask: **Did the result of that story surprise you, or was that easy to believe? Why?**

Why do you think it would be so important for someone to be spoken to and, basically, be loved like those babies needed?

Let group members share their thoughts. Then ask: **On a scale of 1 to 10, how important do you think it is for a human being to feel love and be loved by another human being?**

Let them give their "ratings," and then ask: **On that same scale, how important is it for a person to feel God's love?** Again, get ratings and have people explain their answers.

Leader's Tip: *Be prepared for correct, "churchy" answers, as God's love probably will rate as a "10" for most group members. While hopefully that is true, you may want to make the point that many people in the world only will feel God's love when they feel loved by another human being. It's like the phrase from the Steve Green song that goes, "You're the only Jesus some will ever see. . . ." In other words, human love is usually the vessel to carry God's love to others.*

Discuss together the lists that group members came up with for question one, Section I on page 48 of the journal. Some discussion-starting questions you might throw out to get people going might include: **Were you surprised at the number of people you had on your list when you were finished? Explain. How did you feel after writing out your list? Explain.**

Dig In

To some, the Old Testament is nothing more than a bunch of laws, a bunch of kings, a bunch of stories about war and battles, and several natural disasters all thrown in together. But the Old Testament is based on God's love, an unconditional love that He had for His chosen people, the Israelites.

Get group members' responses to questions one and two in Section II.

1. What is the first thing that comes to your mind when you think of God in the Old Testament?

2. What have you thought about God's toughness/tenderness at different stages of your life? (Child, adolescent, and now.)

You read in your journals about how God chose to love the Israelites in Deuteronomy 7:7, 8. What did you discover about the kind of love God has for you in the passages listed under question five?

Get four volunteers to read the four listed verses, as well as sharing the answers they wrote.

After group members have shared, take a look at questions six and seven. Spend a few minutes dealing

INSIDE INSIGHTS

■ The Bible probably could be compared favorably with recent polls regarding teenage young people's lack of a father-figure, or a mother for that matter. Psalm 27:10 states, "Though my father and mother forsake me, the Lord will receive me." And if recent statistics are correct, there is a good chance that nearly 50 percent of teenage kids come from single-parent families, while the majority of those will be living with mom, not dad. And for the teenagers who do live with their fathers, recent statistics show that most dads spend less than three minutes of meaningful time with their teenage children each day. If teenagers need anything in today's society, they need fathers. Enter God, the loving Father.

■ Psalm 23 may not necessarily seem like a compliment for those who God calls His sheep. Why? Sheep are dumb. In fact, sheep are one of the dumbest animals in the world. They will starve to death unless led to food. They don't have the sense to run from wild animals, and will often stand still while a wolf devours them. They will even follow other sheep off a cliff without a second thought. Face it, sheep need a shepherd. And humans need the Lord as their Shepherd.

with these, as the area of wondering if God's love is conditional or not is a crucial concept in understanding His love.

6. When do you most doubt God's love for you?

7. Do any of the previous verses address your doubts? If so, how?

This might be a good time for you to take the lead in sharing, because answering this question shows vulnerability. For even though people constantly read Bible verses that say how God's love is always there, there are still times when they think, "After what I've done, there's no way God could love me now."

For Christians, a time like that might be when they fall back repeatedly into sin, perhaps like a sinful habit they can't seem to kick. Your sharing will make other people feel more at ease in sharing their doubts. Then, let everyone comment who wants to do so.

Again, let people comment whether or not these verses help them with any doubts. After they've finished commenting, lay on a "clincher verse" that should erase any doubts about God's love.

Ask for someone to read Romans 8:35-39. Discuss the passage together after it's been read. Ask: **How much more do we need to hear? It says that nothing can "separate us from the love of God."**

Take a few minutes to look at the comparative lists of God's love and the world's love that group members came up with for question eight in Section II.

After you've finished discussing the various lists people came up with, say: I **think we can safely say that God's love is quite different than the world's love. Now let's look at a few images or comparisons that the Bible makes in explaining *how* God loves us.**

Rather than taking several minutes to discuss these three images, just ask for volunteers to say what the image is, and how the related Scriptures "define" or portray that love.

Here are the answers to help guide you in case group members get a little stuck or (gasp!) didn't complete their journal for that week.

Image #1—A Father's Love (defined): He has compassion on us, lets us draw close to Him (making Him our "*Abba*" [Daddy]), and disciplines us for our ultimate good.

Image #2—A Shepherd's Love (defined): He provides for us, "pursues" us when we wander off from Him, and protects us.

Image #3—A Husband's Love (defined): He gives up His own rights for us and cares for us.

 ## Reflect and Respond

 Ask group members to take a look at question nine in Section II. Have them think back in their own lives about whether or not they've ever been hurt or disappointed by someone else's love toward them. And if so, in what way?

Encourage those who are willing to share to do so, but don't force anyone. After that time of sharing, "flip the coin" by talking about real love—the love of God.

Say: **God knows the benefits His love can have for us and for all humanity. God wants us to accept and enjoy His love, and to put our hope in it, and share it with others.**

Ask group members to pair up and make a short list of ways that they can: *accept, enjoy, put their hope in, and share with others* God's love.

After a few minutes, bring the groups back together and let them share their lists with the rest of the whole group.

3 Sharing and Prayer

Tell everyone that you're going to read the "Keep In Mind" section, on page 54 of the journal, paying special attention to the story about Karl Barth.

When you're finished, say: **When you think about it, can you think of anything more assuring than knowing that Jesus loves us, because the Bible promises us that it's true?**

Take a few minutes to encourage and uplift each other, or if any group members want to share how this week's study has made a difference in the security they feel in God's unconditional love for them.

Close in prayer to God, thanking Him for His "blanket security" that is available to us through His love. Pray that you and your group members would seek out that security and would have a peace that you would never be separated from the love of God, and that this unconditional love would be a message you would share with others.

Before group members leave, encourage them to complete Week Six in time for your next meeting.

WEEK 6 Baby Grand!

The Coming of Jesus

Overview

• to bring to life the meaning and relevance of the first coming of Jesus Christ.

• to help group members further understand why Jesus came in human form and what our response should be to Christ.

Scripture: selected Scriptures regarding the miracle of Christ's birth and some reasons behind this Incarnation

1 Getting Started

Housekeeping

If any new people have joined your group, make quick introductions, and catch them up on the first five-week unit by reviewing the first five topics. Actually, this review could probably be just as helpful for the "regulars" as well as the "rookies."

In fact, you may want to award a prize to the person who can write down in his or her journal the quickest—both forward and backward—the first five topics your group discussed.

Icebreaking

For this activity, you'll want to have instructed group members the week before to have brought copies of their birth certificates with them this week. If that's not possible, have them ask their parents what their weight and length was when they were born.

Gather in a circle and pass out several small slips of paper to each group member. Explain that for each group member, all of the other group members must guess what that person's weight and length was when he or she was born by writing their guess on a slip of paper and passing them to you, the leader.

You will then read each guess out loud, comparing it to the actual weight and length as stated on the birth certificate or based on what that person tells you.

Award a small prize to the person who guessed the weight the closest, as well as to the person who guessed the length the closest. Let the prizes be "baby-related," like a small jar of baby food, or a pacifier or a diaper, for example.

Be sure to make your guesses for every group member. After you're finished, say: **I wonder what the measurements of Jesus would have been. Who knows, maybe He was the same size as** (one of the guys) **or the same as** (one of the girls). **The fact is, God came to earth as a human being. Let's look at the importance and the whole mystery behind the most important birthday ever known.**

Opening

This could be the ideal time for the group to sing some Christmas carols (even if it's the middle of summer!). Depending on your mood, you could either sing some of the Christian hymns like "Silent Night, Holy Night" or "Joy to the World!", or (if the group's feeling a bit rowdy and lighthearted), you could sing some Christmas favorites like "Deck the Halls" or "Jingle Bells."

Afterward, thank the Lord in prayer for sending His Son to this earth as the ultimate Christmas gift. Also, pray that your group would understand the importance of the birth of Christ, an act that changed the course of history.

2 Bible Study

Focus

This would be a good time to take a step back and get the big picture of what you're wanting to accomplish with this book.

Explain to group members that you've just completed the unit on the Father, looking at an overview of His existence and attributes. Give a quick review by mentioning that the group looked at His proven existence, His awesome power, His sovereign control, His intimidating-yet-intimate holiness, and His faithful love.

Tell everyone that now it's time to look at the second Person of the Trinity, God the Son—Jesus Christ. Explain that in this second unit (Weeks 6-10), you will study His first coming, His life, His death, His resurrection, and His lordship. Before getting into the study, say a quick prayer, asking God to help you see Jesus like you've never seen Him before!

Have group members turn to page 59 in the journal and recruit someone to read out loud the story in Section I, "A Legend for All Times."

After the story's been read, repeat this line of the story: **"If he [Saint Nicholas] were alive today, he no doubt would be surprised at the way his image (among other things) has pushed aside Christ as the focus of Christmas."**

Then ask: **Do you believe that statement is true, that Christ has been pushed aside as the focus of Christmas? Explain.**

After your group has talked about some of the ways Christmas's true meaning seems to have been diluted over the years, explain that now you're going to take an in-depth look at the real Christmas story—the one that took place nearly 2,000 years ago in Bethlehem, and how the various miraculous events in the Christmas story affect your faith today.

Leader's Tip: This week's study will demand thought-provoking questions, unique insights, and fresh new approaches as the Christmas story will no doubt be some-

INSIDE INSIGHTS

thing most of the group members know (or think they know) like the back of their hands. Be creative and enthusiastic with this familiar story. Your zest just might rub off on the others.

Dig In

■ Mary was possibly as young as 13 years old. At that age, she was engaged to be married to a man named Joseph, although to be engaged at such a young age was not unusual in that time and culture. Mary and Joseph's engagement was a much more binding relationship than a modern engagement as it could only be broken by divorce. Though by law they were considered husband and wife, Mary and Joseph did not have sexual relations during their engagement period, and they didn't have sexual relations until after Jesus was born.

■ Although the legal father of Jesus, Joseph is not properly called Jesus' father. In Matthew 1:16, Joseph is called the husband of Mary, from whom was born Jesus. In Luke 2:48, 49, Jesus answers Mary's statement, "Your father [referring to Joseph] and I have been anxiously searching for you," by saying, "Didn't you know I had to be in my Father's [referring to God] house?"

Start off by asking group members to simply call out the things they wrote down for question one in Section II. You might select someone to compile a group list on a sheet of paper. Then have a group member give the answer for question two in Section II. Once the answer has been given, ask for group members who came up with a limerick to share it with the rest of the group.

After any limericks have been shared, this might be a good time to ask: **Why do you think God chose Mary? What was so special about _her_?** Let people respond with their thoughts, but you might try to answer it with two perspectives:

1. God simply chose Mary out of His sovereignty.

2. Mary was the kind of person God takes pleasure in using in mighty ways. She was morally pure, and later in Luke 1, we also find out that she

was a young teenager committed to God's Word. In her spontaneous praise to God (vss. 46-55), it is estimated she made reference to over 15 passages of the Old Testament! Could we do that on a moment's notice?

In Matthew 1:18, 19, Mary realizes she has to tell Joseph about her pregnancy. How did this take courage? Let people offer up their thoughts and suggestions. If no one mentions it, point out that she knew she would probably be ridiculed by others. She knew Joseph could divorce her for this. And she knew the Old Testament well enough to figure out she could be stoned to death for this (Lev. 20:10; Deut. 22:23, 24).

Say: **God chose a virgin to carry His Son in order to doubly confirm that Jesus' birth would be a genuine miracle of God. But why do you think this act is so important and necessary to the Christian faith?**

Let group members wrestle with this question a bit. They'll probably try to explain this phenomenon. After some exhaustive discussion, say: **Some people will argue that not being conceived by a human father wouldn't make Jesus sinless—and therefore qualified to die for our sins—because Jesus still had a human sinning mother. Virgin or non-virgin isn't the issue. They would raise the question, "Why wouldn't Jesus have received a sinful human nature from His mother?"**

Suggest to group members that if they want to look further into this topic, they could read Millard Erickson's *Christian Theology*, particularly pages 154-158. But then stress that the point of God being fully God and fully human isn't to try to explain how this could be.

Have group members turn to page 62 in the journal as your group goes over the answers of the matching exercise in Section III. Here are the answers for the matching exercise: 1–c; 2–a; 3–g; 4–b; 5–f; 6–e; 7–d.

Ask group members what they thought when they read the Old Testament predictions about the birth of Christ, knowing that they were all fulfilled. After they've commented, review Dr. Stoner's comparison about the likelihood of someone fulfilling just 48 of the 300 messianic prophecies that Jesus completely fulfilled.

Ask group members' for their answers to questions two and three in Section IV. Point out that these two questions appear to point to opposite ends of the spectrum. On one end, we see Jesus feeling like any human being would. But on the other, He is God, calming the storm at sea.

Say: **We've studied about Christ's birth—the amazement of it, the likelihood of its being foretold, the wonder of Jesus being both fully God and fully human. But now, we're going to "get to the point"—and I don't mean Cedar Point, either.**

Have group members share the answers they came up with on question four, Section IV. Discuss as a group the importance of these reasons why Jesus came, focusing particularly on Luke 19:10.

 ## Reflect and Respond

Spend some time as a group sharing how you answered question six in Section IV, which asked how can we better worship Christ in today's world.

Refer back to the topic of Christmas once again. Brainstorm together as to what some ways would be to get people to worship God more often than just at Christmas.

Point out that Christmas marks the birth of Jesus, but that His life and His reason for coming aren't tied to just one day. Instead, stress that we should praise and worship God daily for sending His Son—through the virgin Mary—so that we might have eternal life.

3 Sharing and Prayer

Ask the other group members if their mentalities about the Christmas season have changed at all based on the study they've just had. Encourage them to explain any changes in their thinking.

Discuss together some ways that you, as a group, might try to change other people's mentalities about Christmas. Perhaps you could serve at a homeless shelter on Christmas Eve for a few hours. You may still want to bring food, gifts, and a festive spirit, but the real reason could be telling the story of Jesus and the reason for His coming. Brainstorm together for other options.

Close with prayer. Offer an "open-forum" prayer setting, where anyone can pray who feels led. Encourage people to thank God for reminding them of the real reason for the Christmas season, and that they would share this "gift that lasts" with others.

Before group members leave, encourage them to complete Week Seven in time for your next meeting.

WEEK 7 History's MVP

The Life of Jesus

Overview

• to give group members an in-depth look into Jesus' life and its uniqueness.

• to challenge group members to follow Jesus' example.

Scripture: selected passages on the life of Christ and those it impacted

1 Getting Started

Housekeeping

Pass out journals to any newcomers to your group. Once again, remind group members about the key to the journal—MARKING IT UP! Review some of the ways the journal can be used, and also make reference to the contest of who can have the most marked-up journal. Make any necessary announcements.

Icebreaking

Prepare a worksheet for the following matching activity. Pass out copies of the worksheet to everyone, and explain that people must match up the name of the awards with the various descriptions of the awards. The first person to complete the worksheet, sign it, and turn it in to you (the leader) correctly is the winner.

Your job is to arrange the descriptions and answers in two columns. Scramble them up however you want. Feel free to add any more awards you can think of. Award some sort of prize to the winner. Here are the correct matches.

AWARDS	DESCRIPTION
The Academy Awards	Films (Movies)
The Dove Awards	Christian Music
The Caldecott Awards	Best Illustrated Children's Books
The Cy Young Award	Major League Baseball's best pitcher
The Tony Awards	Theater and Broadway
The Addy Awards	Advertising
Heisman Trophy Award	College football's best player
The Emmy Awards	Television
The Grammy Awards	Music
Mr. Universe	World's Top Male Bodybuilder

Opening

Depending on your group's mood or level of rowdiness, you can go a couple of different routes with your singing. If you're a bit more serious, sing the worship chorus, "Jesus, Name Above All Names." But if you're wound up, a song sure to get your group fired up is the Christian contemporary classic, "J-E-S-U-S" by Leon Patillo. Just be sure to bring a portable cassette recorder with you to the meeting.

Once you've finished singing, have a short time of prayer before getting into your study. Here's a prayer you might use or supplement with one of your own.

God, thank You for sending Your Son, Jesus, and for the possibility of eternal life because of Him. Let us leave this meeting time today with a renewed, increased excitement about Jesus Christ, His life, and the impact He made on people's lives and can make on people's lives today. In Jesus' name we pray. Amen.

2 Bible Study

Focus

Ask your group members: **On a scale from 1 to 10, with "1" being low, and "10" being high, how would you rate the importance people in today's society place on winning?**

Give group members a few moments to decide on their ratings, and then let each group member share his or her rating with the rest of the group. People will probably rate fairly high. If so, then ask: **Why do you think society places so much emphasis on winning?** Let group members respond.

When everyone who wants to share has finished, have group members turn to page 67 in the journal, and "volunteer somebody" to read the illustration, "World Series Madness."

Say: **Most of you probably don't remember that great night in baseball that made Reggie Jackson famous. But what, in your lifetime, is the greatest moment in sports—any sport—that sticks out most in your mind where some athlete became famous for it?**

Let group members think for a few minutes as they come up with their greatest moments in sports history. Then let them respond with their answers. But don't force anyone to share who doesn't want to.

Okay, try to return the focus back to the lesson. Say: **If Jesus Christ is indeed history's Most Valuable Person—as [the volunteer who just read] just read, He has to be able to back it up.**

Explain that Jesus has four convincing reasons why He is, indeed, history's MVP:

1. His Words
2. His Works
3. His Walk
4. His Witness

Dig In

Have group members share what they circled in the three passages under question one in Section II. When finished, ask question two in Section II, which asks what Christ Himself said about His words.

Discuss with group members why, despite these claims from Jesus' followers and Christ Himself, why people don't seem amazed at His teaching, but rather bored instead?

Ask group members how they responded personally to question four of Section II. After some have responded, ask: **How were those who first heard Jesus speak different from people today who constantly hear Christ's teachings yet feel bored and don't sense any change in their lives?**

Let group members respond. Here are a few thoughts you might throw out for suggestion.

Those Christians who first heard Jesus speak:

• were willing to be taught

• actually believed what He taught

• paid close attention to Him

INSIDE INSIGHTS

■ A study of the life of Peter is the study of contrast. The Peter most of us know and recall is the Peter who didn't have the courage to stand up for Christ to a little slave girl (Matthew 26:69-75). He was weak, timid, afraid of the crowd. But after seeing Jesus resurrected, Peter became as bold as a lion. There was no one he wouldn't "take on" for Christ, including the Jewish religious establishment (Acts 4:8-13). He even became the church's number one spokesman, standing up at Pentecost and preaching to thousands about Christ (Acts 2:14).

■ The group of people that Paul (then Saul) was persecuting before God changed his life on the road to Damascus actually weren't commonly known as Christians, but as members of "the Way." The Way was one way the Christian church in those years was designated. Regarded as a "sect" by the Romans, the Way is mentioned several times throughout the Book of Acts.

- were hungry for spiritual truth
- no doubt discussed His words amongst themselves
- were hearing a radically new teaching

Assign six people to read the six passages listed in question two in Section III (page 70 of the journal), and answer what miracle Jesus performed in each particular passage.

Which miracle impresses you the most out of all these that we just read about? Why? Give each group member a chance to say which miracle is his or her favorite.

(Section III) 4. Suppose Jesus came to your town today, and you were on the side of the road watching Him pass by. Would you ask Him for a miracle? if so, what would you ask for?

Encourage group members to share their answers, as well as their explanations for the answers regarding the list of miracles on page 70 of the journal. Then say: **It's obvious that Jesus' works speak for themselves. But let's take a look at His next reason in His bid for history's MVP—His walk.**

Explain to the group members that in as much as Jesus was human like the rest of us, He was different from us because He was sinless. But point out that Jesus doesn't boast about His perfect, spotless life; instead, He uses it—for our benefit.

(Section IV) 3. But how does His sinless life relate practically to you today? Recruit four group members to read the passages under question three, and discuss as a group how we are the beneficiaries of Christ's perfection. Say: **These verses show us why we don't need to try to win God over through good works, because Jesus' perfection—which enabled Him to die for our imperfection—already paved the way for us.**

Explain that since you've looked at Jesus' words, His actions, and the way He lived His life, the next thing to look at would be the impact all those things had on others.

Assign three group members to answer questions one through three in Section V. After reading about these people's changed lives, tell group members you want to give them a chance to share any impact Christ has had on them personally.

 Let any group members who are willing to share read their response to question four in Section V to the rest of the group.

Leader's Tip: Be sure to give plenty of affirmation to those willing to share a response like the one in question four, Section V. Divulging how God has changed your life is an extremely vulnerable situation, so don't let anyone get caught up in "getting the low-down" on a particular person. Instead, affirm them and thank them for their contributions.

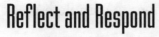 Reflect and Respond

Ask a variation of question five in Section V by asking: **What is happening in your life right now that people could look at and compare that with the way Jesus lived with His life?**

Ask: **Who are some people in your life that you think you might be able to impact for Christ?** Let group members respond.

Afterward, mention the four aspects of Jesus' life that you've looked at—His words, His works, His walk (life), His witness (impact). Then ask question one in the "Keep In Mind" section.

 1. As you look at the life of Jesus, what is one aspect of His life that you want to develop in your own?

Let group members who are willing to share do so, and ask them to explain why that area is the one they want developed.

 2. What is one way you could accomplish this in your life?

To help answer this question, brainstorm together as a group to come up with several ideas that might help them be open to or available for Jesus to help them grow to be more like Him.

3 Sharing and Prayer

Begin this time by taking any prayer requests or listening to any answers of prayer that have taken place. You might offer up a prayer request that everyone in the group would strive to model every area of his or her life life after Christ.

Then, close in prayer by forming a circle around the room. Let each person who is willing read what he or she wrote in the "Pray About It!" section, that said, "Lord, I want to model my life after Yours, especially in . . ."

Designate someone to close the prayer time by thanking God for sending Someone we couldn't ask for to be a better model to pattern our lives after.

Before group members leave, encourage them to complete Week Eight in time for your next meeting.

WEEK 8 — Paid in Full!

The Death of Jesus

Overview

• to clearly communicate both the physical and spiritual perspectives of Christ's death on the cross.

• to help group members understand the spiritual victory obtained through Christ's atoning death.

Scripture: selected passages on the events of the death of Jesus and its significance for humanity

1 Getting Started

Housekeeping

Discuss together as a group how everyone feels about the time and place of each week's meeting. If any changes are desired, make them together as a group. You might want to encourage anyone who is interested in being involved in a leadership role to talk to you after the meeting, since group members have had several weeks to watch you in action and may want to give it a shot as well.

Icebreaking

You'll want some light time before getting into this week's session, so think of a couple of fun games you might want to play. One you might play is the "Never-ending Question Game."

Have group members get in a circle. Explain that the object of the game is in the title—that is, the questions can never end. One person will be designated the leader. He or she will start by asking a person a question. That person must respond back by asking a different question either to the leader or to anyone else in the circle. Then *that* person must ask another question to someone in the circle, and so on and so on.

The point is that a question must be asked every time. The trick is that no question can be repeated, and that the person must ask his or her question in enough time to stay in a rhythm established by the group.

If a person repeats a question, doesn't say something in the form of a question, or takes too long before asking a question, then that person must go to the last seat in the circle. Everyone else moves one seat closer to the leader.

The object is to unseat the leader and become the leader yourself. Play this for several rounds.

Opening

Now is the time you'll want to start bringing the group members' focus back to the theme of your study time. Because they'll still probably be a bit rowdy, a great song that has energy, yet still is about the death of Jesus, is the classic by Petra, "It Is Finished."

Have this serve as your singing time, and ask the group members to listen closely to the words and to try to actually picture what the song is describing. When the song is finished, have everyone bow in prayer. Here's a prayer you might want to use or add to your own.

God, we come reverently before You, thanking You for Your Son and what He did on the cross. May we never lose sight of all the pain and suffering that Jesus went through for us, and the victory it means in our lives today. In Jesus' name. Amen.

2 Bible Study

Focus

Have group members turn to page 75 in the journal and recruit one of them to read Section I, "Shadow of Death." When that's been read, ask: **When you think of a cross, what are some other thoughts that come to your mind other than "what Jesus was crucified on"?**

Let people respond. Here are a few suggestions to add if no one mentions them—something people wear as necklaces, something you find on a church steeple, something you find on a grave, making the cross sign with your fingers like followers of Catholicism do, something in movies that fends off vampires, etc.

Ask: **Do you think most people know the real meaning of what the cross really signifies? Why or why not?** Explain that as a group, you're going to take a detailed look at Christ's suffering and anguish, and the motivation behind His sacrificial act.

INSIDE INSIGHTS

■ The word "Gethsemane" actually means "oil press," or a place where the oil is squeezed out of olives. It is ironic that in Gethsemane, where the oil is squeezed out of olives, that Jesus had His blood squeezed out of Him by stress and internal anguish. Jesus may have suffered from a condition known as "hematidrosis," where tiny blood vessels actually burst and mix with the sweat glands because of extreme emotional duress.

■ The phrase *"It is finished"* is one word in the Greek language. This word is a banking term meaning "a debt has been paid off in full," which is precisely what Jesus' atoning death did. It paid off our sin debt to God, and as a Christian, you don't *owe* God any good work to help pay off your sins. Jesus paid it all. We are to serve God as we have been mandated by Him, and to do so out of love and a desire to serve, not because it's needed to complete what Jesus started.

Dig In

Ask group members for their responses to questions two and three of Section II. Let them respond, but explain that Jesus probably didn't so much dread death, but He did dread the way He would die—as the one who was taking the sins of all humanity on Himself. People may suggest that the "cup" Jesus wanted taken from Him was God's anger toward sin.

Ask: When you think about Jesus sweating drops of blood, how does that make you feel? Let people answer.

How do you think Jesus felt when He returned to His disciples the first time and found them sleeping? What about the second time? The third time? Let group members respond and comment how Jesus must have felt that He couldn't count on the sleepy disciples.

Have group members come up with a modern-day example that might be similar in human failure with the instance of the disciples' falling asleep on Jesus in His greatest hour of need in the garden of Gethsemane. Here's one example:

Chad has been staying with his grandparents in Oregon all summer. His best friends, Justin and Luke, have been back home in Chicago all summer. However, Chad is flying back into Chicago tonight; and Justin and Luke said they would be there to greet him as he comes off the plane, and then they would take him home.

But when Chad gets off the plane, Justin and Luke are nowhere to be found. He waits for several minutes, then decides to call Justin's house. Justin answers the phone, and a surprised Chad asks him why he and Luke aren't at the airport.

Justin replies, "Was that tonight? I'm sorry, we totally forgot about it! Luke's right here; we're on our way!"

Chad waits for another 30 minutes, but still no Justin or Luke. Not knowing what to do, he decides to call Justin's again.

"Hello," says Justin, answering the phone.

"Why are you still sitting there?" asks Chad, irritated.

"Oh I'm sorry," says Justin, "but we were watching this game, and we just lost track of time. But the game's just ending, so we're on our way!"

Chad mumbles a "Hurry up!" and slams down the phone. Yet another 30 minutes later, there's still no Justin and Luke, so Chad takes a cab home. Arriving home, he crawls into bed, penniless—and feeling friendless.

Okay, maybe the examples don't need to be that extensive, but you get the picture. Go around the room, letting group members share their scenarios one at a time.

After you've finished this, review as a group the six trials Jesus faced (you may just want to have six people read about the trials from the journal).

Begin discussing Christ's death, by asking question one in Section IV.

1. How is this beating described (John 19:1-3)?

After someone has answered the question, allow for a few comments on the detailed description of Jesus' physical pain after question one on page 79 in the journal.

Leader's Tip: *Don't try to over-sensationalize the events described in Jesus' suffering. While His suffering is something we can't fathom, some popularizers like to get more vivid than is really needed. Instead, focus on Christ's suffering from a spiritual standpoint as well—deserted by His Father, bearing the sin of all humanity—you don't need to overdo the physical description.*

While Jesus suffered a horrible physical death, He was suffering in the spiritual realm as well. Look at question one in Section V.

1. What was taking place in the spiritual realm as Jesus hung on the cross (II Corinthians 5:21)? Challenge all group members to put their answer into their own words. Ask if any of them want to share their answers out loud.

Reflect and Respond

4. (Section V) Think back to the time that you first understood and accepted Christ's work on the cross. What happened? What did you experience? What impact did it have on you?

Let people respond as they are led to respond. Then ask: **How strong is the meaning about what Christ did for you on the cross in your life right now? Is it stronger and more vibrant, or has it faded?**

Again, let group members respond, and then brainstorm together for some ways to keep that fire—of thanks for being reconciled to God by Jesus—burning hot in your lives.

3 Sharing and Prayer

Take some time to talk together about what Christ's death on the cross did for you in addition to enduring the punishment you deserved for your sin. Look at question three, Section V.

3. As Jesus finished His work on the cross, what else was He accomplishing for us?

Have three members read the three passages, and comment on Christ's accomplishments (i.e., gives us peace and salvation).

Share together if this study time has given you an increased thankfulness to Jesus for paying your debt—the punishment you deserved because of sin.

Close by letting each person in the room personally finish the prayer in the "Pray About It" section, which says, "Lord, when I think about what You did on the cross for me, I . . . ." Before group members leave, encourage them to complete Week Nine in time for your next meeting.

WEEK 9 Gravebuster!

The Resurrection of Jesus

Overview

• to help group members celebrate Christ's victory over death.
• to impart hope and confidence into group members' faith.

Scripture: selected passages depicting both the events surrounding the Resurrection and what it means for Christians

1 Getting Started

Housekeeping

Have another small "forum" time where group members discuss how they feel about the group meeting time itself. Take suggestions that might make the time be more beneficial.

If you have an announcement, make it to the group by acting it out in a game of "charades." Give a small prize to the group member who first translates what the announcement actually is.

Icebreaking

Explain that the resurrection of Jesus is a thorn in the side of many religions that emphatically deny it. To become a bit more familiar with some of these religions, tell group members that you're going to have a word find featuring various religions and their founders.

Say that the first person to correctly complete the word find, sign his or her name to the sheet, and hand in the sheet to you will win some sort of prize. Let group members know that there are 18 clues—nine religions and nine people who founded those religions—that are in the word find.

Have group members write down what they find at the bottom of the page, but explain that they must also try to match up each religion with the person that they think is the religion's founder. Prizes will be awarded both for the person who completes the word find the quickest, and for who matches the most religions/founders correctly.

Creating this word find is your job. Be sure to make the word find difficult, letting some of the words be diagonal, backwards, vertical, horizontal, etc. Below are the clues to mix into your word find. Happy hunting!

Confucius	Confucianism
Buddha	Buddhism
Joseph Smith	Mormonism
Charles Taze Russell	Jehovah's Witnesses
Mary Baker Eddy	Christian Science
Mohammed	Islam
Sun Myung Moon	Unification Church
L. Ron Hubbard	Scientology
Maharishi Yogi	Transcendental Meditation

Opening

An ideal song for your group to sing might be "Shine, Jesus Shine," by Graham Kendrick (© 1987 Make Way Music Ltd., ARR. UBP.). It's a powerful, intense chorus that cries out to Jesus to touch people's lives. It's kind of fitting that it can be sung during one of the most upbeat weekly sessions—the resurrection of Jesus.

Prepare for your study time with a prayer that focuses on praising God that Jesus could overcome sin and death, and for the importance that His resurrection can have in people's lives today.

2 Bible Study

Focus

Have group members turn to page 83 in the journal and recruit one of the group members to read Section I, "End of the Road."

Then ask: **How many of you have ever been to a funeral? What were some of the emotions that you felt? Have you ever been to a funeral that was upbeat?**

Let people share some of their feelings and experiences if they're willing. After everyone's had a chance to share, explain that you're going to be looking today at a funeral that was short-lived—Christ's funeral—because of His resurrection!

Point out that you'll discuss areas like proving to doubters that Christ actually died, actually rose from the dead, and what the Resurrection means to the Christian faith.

Dig In

The first point you'll want to discuss is how some people try to

INSIDE INSIGHTS

■ To say Jesus' tomb was sealed shut is to put it literally. In addition to the large stone sealing off the entrance, the tomb was probably sealed with a cord stretched across the huge stone and sealed on each side of the tomb with wax. The wax would be impressed with the seal of the Roman government. Any movement of the stone would be easily detected.

■ When there was a violent earthquake and an angel of the Lord came and rolled the stone away from the tomb (Matthew 28:2), it says in verse four that the guards were so afraid of him that they shook with fear and then passed out. The Greek root word for "shook" in verse four is the same Greek root as the word for "earthquake" in verse two. In other words, the guards had a case of the "shakes."

refute Jesus' resurrection by saying He actually never died. Ask your group members to respond with any evidence they found in the Scripture passages listed under question one, Section II.

1. How do these verses describe Jesus' death?

• Matthew 27:50

• John 19:32-35

• Mark 15:44, 45

Let people respond with their answers, and say something along these lines: **We've read that the Bible says He died, and we believe it to be historically accurate. The soldiers proved He died because they didn't break His legs, which was done to *quicken* death. Medicine says He died based on the blood and water that flowed when His body was pierced by the spear. This indicated His pericardium and the heart itself were both ruptured, which results in death. And the centurion, who had the final say on whether someone was dead, told Pilate that Jesus was dead. Pretty convincing stuff, huh?**

Mention the things that the journal lists that happened when Jesus died. Ask: **How would you have felt if you had witnessed tombs breaking open and believers who had died coming back to life? Do you think this is an event that is forgotten or overlooked when people think of Jesus' death? Explain.**

Let group members share their responses.

Point out that Jesus' tomb was protected by Roman soldiers, as well as by a huge stone that was sealed across the tomb's entrance. This was to prevent anyone from stealing His body and claiming He was alive again.

Have someone read the story of Ehrich Weiss (Harry Houdini) in Section III on page 85 of the journal.

Ask group members if any of them can perform magic tricks. If someone can, give the person a coin and see if he or she can make it disappear (unless they happen to have a few tricks with them!). Then explain that Jesus performed the ultimate magic trick, but it wasn't an illusion—it was real! Jesus is actually alive after really dying.

As a group, go over the answers you came up with for questions one through five in Section III as you discuss the action that occurred when Jesus was nowhere to be found!

Discuss together the ridiculousness of the story the priests and elders had the guards make up. Refer to the journal where it points out all the holes in the story, particularly the fact how the guards were able to know it was the disciples who stole Jesus' body when they were *asleep*.

(Section III) 7. What emotions would you have felt if Jesus had appeared to you?

After people respond with their thoughts, explain that you want to look at why Christ's resurrection is so important to the Christian faith.

Divide people into three groups, and assign each group a section (A, B, or C) of Section IV. Have group A read the promises of the Resurrection; have group B go over the eyewitnesses of the resurrected Christ they discovered based on the listed passage; and have group C go over the implications they found in the listed passage. Then have each group share its findings with the rest of the group.

Reflect and Respond

Recruit one of your members to read the brief story about General Wellington and the battle of Waterloo under the "Keep In Mind" section on page 89 of the journal.

When finished, point out that the bottom line of the Resurrection is that people have victory—eternal victory—in their lives, when it seemed at first that sin and death had won at the cross.

Have group members discuss the answers they came up with from the Scripture passages in the "Keep In Mind" section about what Jesus' resurrection means in their lives.

A good thing to wrap up your reflect time would be to play the old Carman song, "Sunday's On the Way." This powerful, yet humorous song describes the victory that Christ's resurrection made available for all humanity.

3 Sharing and Prayer

Close by having group members think of one area of their lives where they tend to become discouraged. Then ask them to write down how Christ's resurrection can make a difference in that area of their life. Or ask them to apply this question to their troubling area. **How does the Resurrection give you hope, comfort, confidence, and assurance of victory in this area?**

Encourage people to open up to the other group members about these areas. Ask group members to consider finding an accountability partner to help keep them feeling victorious in their lives—even in difficult circumstances—by remembering Christ's resurrection.

Close with a prayer of thankfulness to God for the victory we have because of Jesus' resurrection. Pray that we live a victorious life, knowing that sin and death and Satan have already been defeated. Also, pray that the Resurrection would serve to strengthen us in our daily battles—knowing the war has already been decided.

Before group members leave, encourage them to complete Week Ten in time for your next meeting.

WEEK 10 Who Do You Say That I Am?

The Deity of Jesus

Overview

• to enable group members to defend the deity of Christ.
• to challenge group members to submit to the lordship of Christ.

Scripture: selected passages affirming the belief of Jesus as God

1 Getting Started

Housekeeping

After this meeting, you will have finished the *second* unit in this book. Once again, decide as a group whether or not you want to take a week off before heading down the homestretch. If you do, be sure to *frequently* remind group members of the break in the action.

You may also want to plan together to meet in a different, unique place for your next meeting. Some meeting place ideas might include at a park, or at a pool for a pool party if one of your group members' families has one. This might liven up your meeting time and give it the fresh twist it may need.

Icebreaking

Here's an activity that will let group members get to know each other's interests a bit better, while also focusing on the topic of your meeting time.

Tell your group members that they are to write down their "list of greatests." That is, what they think is the greatest food, the greatest musician or music group, the greatest place to go for vacation, the greatest food, the greatest movie, the greatest sport, and so on. Supplement this list with some of your own categories, if desired.

After group members have made their lists, go around and have them, one at a time, read one or two examples from their list to the rest of the group. There is one catch, however. Group members must briefly explain, or defend, those choices to the others because the odds are probably pretty good that everyone in the group won't have the exact same list.

This could be a good exercise in making people logically think through the statements and choices they make. Be sure to act impartial and unbiased toward each group member. Give everyone a chance to read his or her list.

Opening

A song you might sing that makes a statement about who Jesus is would be the praise chorus, "Lord, I Lift Your Name on High" by Rick Founds (© 1989 Maranatha! Music. ICS. ARR. UBP.). The chorus clearly explains the progression that Jesus took—from heaven to earth, from the earth to the cross, from the cross to the grave, from the grave to the sky—that clearly says He is our Savior and Lord.

Say a short prayer, asking God that your group members will have it made crystal clear to them that Jesus is Lord and that they would be able to effectively communicate that truth to others.

2 Bible Study

Focus

Have group members turn to page 91 in the journal, while you read the story in Section I about Muhammad Ali.

Ask: **What did you think of Ali's boastful comments? If you were one of Ali's boxing opponents, how would you have felt? If you play sports, how do you feel when your opponent acts all cocky before competing against you and takes you lightly?**

Ask group members if they can think of any other athletes or famous people who have made claims that they didn't back up. For example, maybe some player guaranteed his or team would win a title and it didn't happen, or someone guaranteed he would become governor and didn't get elected.

Afterward, mention that most people enjoy rubbing someone else's face in the dirt when that person boasted about something, but couldn't back it up.

Point out that in Jesus' day, the Pharisees and Jewish officials wanted nothing more than to rub Jesus' face in the dirt when He indicated that He was God or equal with God. But also point out that unlike Muhammad Ali, Jesus backed up every one of His claims.

Let your group members know that similarly, if they witness to others about God, they may be forced to back up their claims about why they believe in God by explaining *why* they believe it ("it" being the deity of Jesus).

Say: **Let's take a look at and try to answer some questions surrounding the idea of Jesus as God.**

Leader's Tip: Encourage group members not to be embarrassed to ask any questions they might have. Wanting to be clear in what one believes and one's ability to defend that belief are very important. You can help others avoid embarrassment by stating that you also have questions, and that asking them shows a desire to learn and grow.

I N S I D E
INSIGHTS

■ The apostle Paul had no trouble claiming that Jesus was indeed God. In Colossians 1:19, he states that Jesus was 100 percent fully God. In fact, in Paul's 13 letters (the Pauline epistles), Paul calls Jesus "Lord" nearly 200 times!

■ The apostle John, referred to in the Gospel of John as "the disciple whom Jesus loved," must have had a great memory. One of the key figures who wrote that Jesus was indeed God, John didn't end up writing his Gospel until close to *60 years* after Jesus had risen from the dead and ascended into heaven. Now that's "total recall"! But the reality of Jesus' deity must still have been fresh in John's mind (we hope! Picture John thinking, "Now was that *He* is the vine, *we* are the branches, or *we* are the vines, *He* is the branch?").

Dig In

You need to turn to the "I am" statements after question one in Section II (page 92 in the journal) but tell your group members not to look in their journals.

Recruit eight group members, and explain that they must act out, "charade-like," the "I am" statement that their Bible verse describes.

Assign the eight passages in John, and then give your new actors and actresses a minute or two to decide what they're going to do. Then, one at a time, have them act out their verse, while the other group members try to guess what the "I am" statement is.

For example, "I am the bread of life," "I am the light of the world," are a few of the easier ones. But "I am the gate for the sheep," "I am the vine," and "I am the way and the truth and the life" might be a bit more difficult.

Be sure to applaud all the participants for their "auditions."

Say: **Now that we've read how Jesus has said He was a lot of things that other people equated only with God, let's see how He backed up these claims.**

Discuss the answers you came up with for question one of Section III. If desired, assign a couple of group members to read the two passages listed under question one.

Ask: Do you think you would have been convinced that Jesus was God just by Him telling the paralytic, "Son, your sins are forgiven" (realizing only God can forgive sin)? Why or why not?

Call on group members to finish the sentences in question two of Section III, regarding some of the miracles of God. Ask: **Do you think you would have been convinced Jesus was God after seeing Him heal the paralytic? Why or why not? Do you think the Pharisees and leaders and officials were convinced? Explain.**

Ask: **If any of those miracles would have convinced you that Jesus was God, which one of the four just mentioned do you think would have convinced you the easiest? Why?**

Explain that now you're going to look at what the people who knew Jesus best said about Him. People like the apostles Peter, James, and John who spent nearly all their time with Him.

Try this little exercise that lets group members see what other group members who know them best would say about *them*.

Have each group member pick the person in the group that he or she thinks knows them best. (Granted, every group member may not have his or her best friend in the group. But after nine weeks together as a small group, hopefully they've developed some type of relationship with some other group members.)

You (the leader) must think of a few categories such as temper, sense of humor, etc. Explain that on a scale of 1 (being low) to 10 (being high), group members must rate themselves in each category. The person each group member picked as their "closest confidant" must also rate the group member in each category. Have people do this by writing down their ratings on a piece of paper.

Going around the room one at a time, have each "pair" share their predictions. Notice how close (or far away) group members are from each other in what they said about the other person. Award prizes to the pair whose predictions were the most similar.

Say: **The people listed in Section IV probably knew Jesus a little bit better than we've just showed in our "knowledge" of each other. But they weren't rating His temper or sense of humor. They were saying that He was God. Let's read exactly what they were saying.**

Assign group members to the characters in Section IV, and discuss together the answers they came up with from reading the passages.

Reflect and Respond

Tell group members that we've seen an abundance of support that Jesus is God. Jesus' words, His works, the words of others, the backing of Scripture—the case is strong.

But stress that it's people like you—in today's society—who still aren't fully convinced.

Review the support for the belief that Jesus is God by looking at the 13 claims in Section V that support He is God.

Let them discuss the first question at the end of Section V (listed below).

Why do you Christians know your religion is the only right one? Have a little testing time that will let group members work at defending their belief that Jesus is God. Have one of your more competent group members serve as someone who is questioning the other group members' beliefs.

Randomly call on some group members to try to defend and explain why their religion is the right one. Make sure they put away their "cheat sheets" (the 13 claims in Section V). Encourage group members when they get stumped trying to answer something. Also encourage people to jot down the answers that others give, as they can use this time to gain insight from each other as well.

When finished, ask group members if any of them are willing to share their answers to the questions in the "Keep In Mind" section.

3 Sharing and Prayer

Ask group members how studying this issue together has strengthened their faith in Christ. Let any respond, if willing.

Mention the following practical ways to apply the truth of Jesus' deity to our lives.

1. Because He is God, I will love Jesus supremely (Matthew 22:37).
2. Because He is God, I will obey Jesus completely (John 14:15).
3. Because He is God, I will share Him openly (Matthew 28:18-20).

Encourage them to come up with one way to implement at least one of these responses into their lives. Close by asking if any group members are willing to share the D-E-I-T-Y acrostic prayer they wrote in the "Pray About It" section. Also, take any prayer requests people might have and close by thanking God for making the issue of Jesus' deity a clearer and more intense area in your Christian lives.

Before group members leave, encourage them to complete Week Eleven in time for your next meeting.

WEEK 11 He's Holy, But He's No Ghost!

The Person of the Spirit

Overview

• to familiarize group members with the Person of the Holy Spirit and His place in the Trinity.

• to help group members see how the Holy Spirit can minister in their lives.

Scripture: selected Bible passages describing the characteristics and the works of the Person of the Holy Spirit.

1 Getting Started

Housekeeping

If any new people have joined the group, scold them for missing the first two units (just kidding!). Actually, give them journals and award a prize to the group member who can list the topics of the first 10 weeks. Answer any questions the newcomers might have.

Encourage group members to try out the leader's role for one of the upcoming weeks, and make any necessary announcements.

Icebreaking

After ten weeks of studying about God the Father and God the Son, your group members may need to be re-energized. This is especially true since this unit covers the Holy Spirit—perhaps the most important Person of the Trinity in the *daily* life of the believer, but the Person most believers know the least about.

So before you get into this new material, play a game of "Name That Tune." Bring a portable stereo and several tapes or CDs. Explain that you're just going to start playing a song at random. The first group member to yell out the title of the song and it's artist is the winner.

Have several songs (some very obscure, some very recognizable) ready to play. You might want to throw a small candy bar or a sucker to group members when they correctly guess a song.

Spend the remaining time munching on the rest of the candy (if there's any left) and letting some of the music play while everyone hangs out for a few minutes.

Opening

A song you may want to sing would be the praise chorus (from Psalm 51) "Create in Me a Clean Heart." The song refers to the Holy Spirit and His intention to dwell in us when it says, "Cast me not away, from Thy presence O Lord; take not Thy Holy Spirit from me. . . ." This song could set the tone for your meeting time.

Say a prayer that asks God for clear minds as you dig into finding out about the Holy Spirit, who exactly He is, and the valuable importance He can have in people's lives.

2 Bible Study

Leader's Tip: Be enthusiastic! At this point in a 15-week study, group members can lose their sense of "freshness" and joy in meeting together. That's why even though all 15 chapters are related, it's best to present them as if they were three five-week units.

Focus

Ask: **What's the hardest class you've ever taken?** Let every group member respond. **How did you feel about taking it? Did you ever feel like you didn't understand much that was being said? Explain.**

After a few minutes of discussion time, state that the idea of the Holy Spirit as the third Person of the Trinity probably makes many people feel the same way they did in that impossible class at school.

Explain that many people have a hard time understanding the Holy Spirit for many reasons. First, you can't picture Him like you could picture Jesus, because He's a spirit. Secondly, people either focus on the Holy Spirit too much or hardly at all, to the point where we don't understand who He really is and what He can do for us.

Explain to group members that the purpose of these final five chapters is to find the proper focus on the Holy Spirit and to understand how to experience His ministries in their lives. But mention that first, you need to figure out exactly who the Holy Spirit really is.

Go over the answers to question one in Section I by having group members call out names of movies they wrote down that have been made about ghosts.

Afterward, ask for any group members who are willing to share their thoughts on how they would describe the Holy Spirit to do so.

Dig In

Explain to the group members that your first task is to explain that the Holy Spirit is a Person, and not a "force" or some ethereal mist. Before anyone can look at his or her journal, ask a group member to tell you what makes a person . . . well, a person—as in, different from an animal.

Let someone answer (you're looking for the idea that a person has intellect, emotion, and will).

INSIDE INSIGHTS

■ If you sang the song, "Spirit of the Living God," in the 1600s, it probably would have sounded a little awkward. During those days, the King James Version (published in 1611) was the Bible most often used, and it referred to the Spirit as a "Ghost." In those days, the two words were used interchangeably. But today, a certain mental image is conjured up when we hear the word "ghost." And besides, the Holy Spirit is a spirit, not a ghost. Can you hear yourself singing, "Ghost of the Living God, fall fresh on me . . ."?

■ The actual word "Trinity" isn't found in the Bible, although it's doctrine is essentially taught in the Scripture. The word "Trinity" was a word created by a second-century theologian to help him better understand the "Tri-unity" of God. Actually, there are many Christian words and phrases not found in the Bible, such as "divine attributes," "deity," and "omniscience," but Christians still believe in them.

Discuss together the answers group members came up with for questions one through five in Section II. Assign people to read the Scriptures that support these claims of the Holy Spirit having these qualities.

Move into Section III, and recruit two people to read the Scripture passages that follow the two phrases, "The Spirit is equal with _____ ." Ask for the answers that will fill in the two blanks (Jesus and God).

Say: **So the Bible indicates the Holy Spirit is equal with God. What are some things about God that the Holy Spirit also is? And what are some things that God does that the Holy Spirit does as well?**

Take a few minutes and review the rest of Section III regarding the characteristics and acts of God that the Holy Spirit also shares. Read the given Bible passages if time allows.

Say: **Earlier, we stated that the Holy Spirit is equal with God the Son and with God the Father. Now we're going to talk about something you may or may not have heard discussed before—the Trinity.**

Have people try to state definitions for the word Trinity. After group members have stated some definitions, ask a few questions that may start some discussion. Don't worry about whether or not you have the correct answer straight from God Himself.

Ask: Can a person be a Christian and not believe in the Trinity? Do you think the disciples knew there was a Trinity?

Let group members banter back and forth. Then state that the Bible states that there is only one God, but He exists in three Persons—the Father, Son, and Holy Spirit. And together, they make up the Trinity. You could illustrate the concept of the Trinity by saying it is like water. Water exists in three states, solid (ice), liquid, and gas (steam). But it is still one substance. Though no illustration is really good enough, it might help clarify this teaching a little.

 Go over the explanations of what the Trinity is not in Section IV to help make the concept a little clearer.

An activity that would maybe bring this concept closer to home for your group members would be to have them act out the different theories of what the Trinity is not. Divide people into three groups, with one group for each different theory. Encourage groups to be creative and funny.

For example, with the theory that the Trinity is three roles played by one person, you could have someone "act out" three roles in a movie. A guy and a girl could be over at the girl's house on a romantic date, when the girl's jealous ex-boyfriend bursts onto the scene and doesn't like what he sees. The challenge is for one of your group members to act out the scene all by himself or herself.

Another example would be the theory which states that the Trinity is three gods functioning together like a team (which is actually polytheism).

You could have three group members act like they are a basketball team. Have another group member announce the "starting lineup" as they run out onto the "court."

 Afterward, explain that the Trinity, though not specifically mentioned by name in the Bible, is referred to in some passages of Scripture. Have group members read the last four passages in Section IV aloud to the group.

Reflect and Respond

Take a little time and review together what you've learned about who the Holy Spirit actually is, and if it's made His relationship with God the Father and Jesus any clearer in your minds.

You might want to encourage group members to think of the Holy Spirit as their "personal Jesus." Point out that since Jesus is no longer here on earth in human form to be with us, we now have the Holy Spirit to be with us as Jesus was with the disciples in His day.

Tell the group members that in the next four weeks you're going to be looking at several questions concerning the Holy Spirit. Give a brief preview by referring to the questions listed in the "Keep In Mind" section on page 105 of the journal.

Say: **If you think of any other questions you might have in the coming week, write them down and bring them to next week's meeting time.**

3 Sharing and Prayer

Take a little time for group members to share their feelings on the study time, and if they thought it was effective. Do they feel like everyone understands who the Holy Spirit really is but them?

Be sure to reassure group members that it's okay to feel a little "in the dark" about this subject. Stress that God doesn't ask us to figure Him out, and that He says in His Word that we can't completely anyway (Isaiah 55:8, 9). Some things we just have to accept by faith.

Close by thanking God that we have such a direct access to Him and His Son Jesus through the Holy Spirit. Pray that the "mystery" of who He is and what He can do in our lives will be made clearer and clearer to the group in the weeks to come.

Before group members leave, encourage them to complete Week Twelve in time for your next meeting.

WEEK 12 Fire from Heaven!

The Coming of the Spirit

Overview

• to learn what the Bible says about the Spirit's presence and empowerment in the lives of believers.

• to help group members experience the personal presence and power of the Holy Spirit in their lives.

Scripture: selected Scriptures regarding the coming of the Holy Spirit into the lives of believers.

1 Getting Started

Housekeeping

Bring in a dozen (or more) doughnuts to your meeting, and mention to everyone that you did it because this week marks the "dozenth" (that's 12th) meeting time you've had. Make any announcements and check if there are any special twists or changes the group would like to incorporate into the last three weeks.

Icebreaking

Tell group members you want them to think about birthday and Christmas gifts they have received over the course of their lifetimes. Instruct them to write down—either on scratch paper or in their journals (preferably in their journals, which will help them in their quest to win the prize for the "most marked-up" journal)—some of the more unusual gifts they've received.

You can make this more structured by coming up with different categories. Some could be:

- Weirdest gift
- Most useless gift
- Cheapest gift
- Most expensive gift
- Least favorite gift
- Most favorite gift

Discussing one gift category at a time, go around the room, and let all group members share their gift for that category with the rest of the group.

For each category, have group members vote on which person's gift depicted that category the best (i.e., which one was the cheapest, the weirdest). Award a prize to the group member whose gift was the "winner" for each category.

 ## Opening

A good worship song that could get your group focusing on God, His Son, and the Spirit would be "Father, I Adore You." Be sure to sing the other two verses, "Jesus, I Adore You," and "Spirit, I Adore You."

You may also want to sing the chorus in a round, where you would divide your group into three sections and have them begin singing the song at different times. When done a cappella-style, this song is very worshipful.

Spend a few minutes in prayer, thanking God for His Spirit which He has sent to dwell in you, and that you would be transformed by the power that His Spirit can place in your lives.

2 Bible Study

Focus

Have group members turn to page 107 in the journal and recruit one of them to read the list of gifts under Section I, "Extra-Special Gift."

Discuss together the extremeness of those gifts, and compare them to some of the unusual gifts that your group members mentioned. After you've finished discussing those gifts, say: **God has given humanity a very special gift that does much more for us than a llama and lasts longer than dinner with a celebrity—sorry Kevin Costner fans. It's the gift of the Holy Spirit.**

Let's look together at how, when, and why God sent the Holy Spirit to us.

Dig In

Say: **Promises are a funny thing—easy to make, but hard to keep. Why do you think that statement is true for so many people?**

INSIDE INSIGHTS

■ In the New Testament, the Greek word for "wind" and "Spirit" is the same, making wind a natural symbol and metaphor for the Holy Spirit. Besides wind, other symbols that refer to the Holy Spirit include "breath," "dove," "fire," and "finger of God."

■ The day of Pentecost was quite a "widespread revival meeting"! Tens of thousands of Jews from at least 16 different regions, representing numerous language groups, were present and were all spoken to in their native tongues by the disciples—through the power of the Holy Spirit.

Let people respond with their thoughts on the difficulty of keeping promises.

Then have group members turn in their journals to question one, Section II on page 108, and share their lists of promises made to them by others that have either been kept or broken. But don't force anyone to share.

After sharing, move on to question five in Section II.

5. Think of a time when someone broke a promise made to you. How did it make you feel toward that person?

Let people discuss their feelings about their experiences for a few moments, and then refer to question two, Section II.

2. Jesus Christ, the ultimate Promise-Keeper, made a promise to His disciples. What was it (John 14:16, 17)? Have someone answer the question, and then get someone to read that Scripture passage.

Comment on how the disciples decided to take Jesus up on that promise by gathering in a large room where they waited and prayed (Acts 1:12-14). Ask: **When you desire something of God, is praying to Him and waiting on Him the natural thing for you to do? Explain.**

Say: **Regarding this promise that Jesus made, what do you think the Holy Spirit would be able to do that Christ was unable to do** (question four, Section II)?

Let group members offer responses. Here's a hint you might offer to them. Ask them to think of some ways that Jesus was limited in His human body.

The main answer you're looking for is that because Jesus was acting within His human body, He experienced normal human limitations concerning His disciples (i.e., when Jesus went off to the garden of Gethsemane and to the unknown mountain where the Transfiguration took place [Matthew 17; Mark 9], He took with Him Peter, James, and John—the disciples who were especially close to Him. This meant that other disciples like Philip, Bartholomew, and Simon the Zealot weren't present with Him during that time).

Based on these facts, state that the advantage of Jesus going to heaven and the Spirit coming to earth is that *everyone* can have a *personal* relationship with God.

To bring the point just a little bit closer to home, offer this little example.

Let's say you're at the Upset Stomach Amusement Park. You're waiting—with seemingly millions of others—for your chance to ride the park's new roller coaster—the biggest, fastest, scariest, wildest ride ever built. The only problem? Having to stand in line for three hours for a chance to ride.

That's like Jesus. He was popular. People flocked, fought, or climbed trees like Zaccheus just to get a glimpse of Him, or just to touch His cloak in the case of the woman who had been bleeding for 12 years. But many people probably never got a chance to see Him, or to "ride that new ride."

But when God sent the Holy Spirit to replace Jesus after Jesus arose, it became like having your own *personal* roller coaster—with no lines! And what's more, having one's "own roller coaster" is available to everybody!

Take a few minutes and encourage group members to try to think of examples or metaphors that will make a similar point about everyone potentially having a personal, direct, and close relationship with God. Let group members share what they come up with.

Another advantage for sending the Holy Spirit comes straight from the mouth of Jesus. In John 14:12, He says the Holy Spirit would come so His disciples could do "greater things" than He did.

Explain that by "greater," Jesus meant greater in extent and scope. To clarify this, point out that if Jesus was preaching in Galilee, nobody was being ministered to by Him in Capernaum. But with believers having access to Christ's power through the Holy Spirit, people could be ministered to in more places than one (i.e., greater ministry).

Have a group member read Acts 2:1-4, and then have people write down what the disciples heard, saw, and did. Discuss this occurrence together.

Leader's Tip: Be sensitive to group members' feelings about this occurrence at Pentecost, as some of them may feel spooked about it. This means talking through people's feelings and impressions about this occurrence, and about the real power of God's Spirit.

Ask: How do you think you would react if you were in a room with several people when you suddenly heard a violent wind, saw flames of fire resting on the other people, and everyone began speaking in different languages? How do you think the disciples and the 120 gathered in that room felt?

Discuss as a group what the three passages listed under question one in Section III have to do with Acts 2:1-4.

After you've discussed those passages together, have a group member answer question three in Section III.

3. According to Jesus, what would be the purpose of this display of power (Acts 1:8)?

Now point out that you're going to look at how that day of Pentecost has paved the way for people like you today. As a group, discuss questions two, three, and five in Section IV.

Reflect and Respond

Say: **We know that the Holy Spirit comes to live inside us the moment we ask God for salvation (Romans 8:9). But we still sometimes struggle, don't we?**

(Section IV) 8. Has there ever been a time when you felt like God had left you, or like He was far away? If so, what did it feel like?

Remind group members that you're not going to force them to share, but that you would encourage them to do so. After any responses, look together at question nine in Section IV.

9. What two evidences do you have that the Holy Spirit will stay in you (John 14:15-18, 23; Romans 8:16)?

Point out that these are promises from God, the ultimate Promise-Keeper. And all that is required of us is to obey His teachings and commands out of our love for Him.

7. (Section IV) What are some of the benefits of having God's presence?

- Deuteronomy 31:6

- Psalm 21:6

3 Sharing and Prayer

Spend some time together, asking each other if you feel the benefits described in your life. If not, explain, and try to think of some steps to take to experience the goodness of God's constant presence in our lives.

Go around your group one person at a time, asking group members to share one way this week's study time has either drawn them closer to God's Spirit living inside of them, or has helped them make more sense of how, when, and why the Holy Spirit has come for those who accept Christ.

Close by asking group members to share the acrostic prayers that they came up with in the "Pray About It" section. Let everyone share who wants to and then close with prayer, reminding group members that God is there with them, in each one of them.

Before group members leave, encourage them to complete Week Thirteen in time for your next meeting.

WEEK 13 The Illuminator

The Ministry of the Spirit

Overview

• to expose group members to the various ministries of the Holy Spirit in their lives.

• to have group members' spiritual needs met through these ministries.

Scripture: John 16:8-15; Romans 3:10-12; other selected passages regarding the ministries of the Holy Spirit

1 Getting Started

Housekeeping

Quickly meet together with some of the others who have led the small group and choose the next topic in the discipleship series, *The Main Thing*. Also, encourage any group members who haven't yet led a meeting time to try their hand at leading one of the last two weeks. Make any needed announcements.

Icebreaking

Try to get your hands on a Swiss Army pocket knife to show to the other group members. Have some fun passing the knife around as everyone gets a good look at the many gadgets and accessories (such as a screwdriver, blade, can opener, corkscrew, scissors, etc.).

One thing you might do is have group members try to guess the function of each gadget you point to on the knife. (Obviously, some of the gadgets are fairly clear as to what their function is, but the functions of some of the other gadgets are up for grabs!)

Another activity would be to have group members finish this phrase: If I were shipwrecked on a deserted island, I would use the _____ function on the knife to _____ .

Randomly select group members and then select one of the functions on the knife (for example, the screwdriver). That group member must state what he or she would use the screwdriver for on the island. Do this for as many group members as the knife has different functions.

When you're finished, point out that just as the one knife has many different functions, the one Holy Spirit performs many different ministries in our lives.

Opening

A good song that focuses on the Spirit working in the lives of Christians would be "Spirit of the Living God (Fall Fresh on Me)." Focus particularly on the lines that plead with the Spirit to minister in the lives of believers—"Melt me, mold me, fill me, use me."

After singing, have a time of prayer. Be sure to spend some of your prayer time in thanksgiving to God for sending us His Spirit who "goes to bat for us" by trying to bring us closer to God. Pray that you would become aware of other ministries and areas that the Spirit wants to develop in the lives of believers.

2 Bible Study

Focus

Ask group members what they thought of the story about the "world-famous explorer," Jacobus Jonker. Let them respond with their thoughts. You might even ask: **Why do you think Mr. Jonker would walk around in the mud after each rain?**

Ask people if their Bible study time is similar to what was described in this section. Are they like a Mr. Jonker, just stumbling around in the Bible and hoping to bump into a nugget of truth? Let those respond who are willing.

Say: **God didn't send the Holy Spirit just to "hang out" with us when we became Christians.** Explain that you're going to see how the Spirit ministers to Christians as well, by specifically looking at:

What He was doing in their lives *before* they were saved; what He does *at the moment* of salvation; and what He *presently* does in Christians.

Dig In

Ask group members for their impressions regarding the story about then Vice President Bush and the Secret Service. Ask if any of them have ever seen a president or vice president in person, or saw where Secret Service agents were protecting someone. Let group members respond. Then ask question one in Section II.

1. What was the Holy Spirit's ministry to you before you became a Christian (John 16:8)? Let group members discuss the answer, and then have someone read verses 16:9-11 as well.

How do you think making people feel convicted and guilty about their sinful lives is considered a ministry?

Have someone read the passage Romans 3:10-12, and then say: **After**

INSIDE
INSIGHTS

■ Many Christians would be quick to agree that sometimes the Bible can be difficult to understand. But they don't often recognize that God sent the Holy Spirit to help us understand the Bible. John 16:13 states that the Spirit will "guide [us] into all truth," referring to God's Word. And I Corinthians 2:10-13 states that the Spirit knows the "deep things" and "thoughts of God" and is qualified to teach us "spiritual truths." A Christian's job is to study God's Word with an open heart. The Spirit's part is to teach us its truths.

■ One person who had something in common with the Spirit was John the Baptist. Like the Spirit, John's main goal was to glorify Jesus, and could be summed up in His statement, "He [Jesus] must become greater; I must become less" (John 3:30). No wonder Jesus called him the greatest man who ever lived (Matthew 11:11). John the Baptist was even filled with the Holy Spirit while still in his mother's womb (Luke 1:15)!

reading this passage, we should be thankful that the Holy Spirit does convict us, since the passage states that no one is righteous. So like the journal said, the result of this ministry is that we are brought to Christ—because of the Spirit's convicting.

Ask: **What do you think are some different ways that the Spirit might convict us?** Let people answer. A few answers to look for would be through other people, emotions, circumstances, but most importantly, God's Word.

Now explain that you're going to look at how the Spirit ministers to people the moment they become Christians. Ask those who would be willing to share to describe how they became Christians—as in when did it happen, where, how old, what God seemed to be saying to them, etc.

Leader's Tip: *Be sure not to make people feel uncomfortable if they don't know the exact details concerning their conversion experiences. Some people may feel that others doubt the validity of their salvation if they can't recall it exactly like it happened yesterday. Don't fuel that doubt.*

Say: **Regardless of whether or not all people's salvation experiences are as clear as a bell, the Spirit still ministers to them by giving them things when they become a Christian. Let's look at a few.**

 Divide group members into three subgroups. Have the three subgroups discuss their answers to questions one through six under Section III regarding a Christian's new beginning, new identity, and new assurance. After each group has discussed its respective section together, have groups reconvene and share what they discussed.

Ask: **How does it make you feel when you're described as a son or daughter of God and a member of His household?**

Let group members share any responses, and then ask: **Based on what we've learned about our assurance, how would you respond to a believer who is doubting that he or she is sealed by the Spirit?** Let group members respond; then explain that now you're going to focus on how the Holy Spirit can minister in Christians' lives on a daily basis.

Again, break up into subgroups, this time dividing into four of them, having them discuss their answers to the questions in Section IV regarding a new direction, new understanding, new closeness, and new motivation. Again, after each group has discussed its respective section together, have the groups reconvene and share what they discussed.

Afterward, ask: **How does it make you feel knowing that the Spirit leads you and intercedes with God for you?**

Reflect and Respond

As a group, go over the "Keep In Mind" section on page 122 of the journal that showed the results available to believers because of the Spirit's ministry in various areas of their lives.

Encourage group members to share which result(s) they think they need the most currently in their lives, and why they feel that way. Don't force anyone to share, however.

After people have shared, brainstorm together as a group to think of some actual practices that group members could use to achieve better results in various spiritual areas. Then encourage them to take those necessary steps.

3 Sharing and Prayer

Have some group sharing time, by having group members answer this question: **What do you think is the most important thing you've learned about the Holy Spirit in this chapter?** Go around the room one at a time, letting each group member share, if desired.

Close your time in prayer by letting group members share the prayers they wrote from the "Pray About It" section. Divide up evenly so each of the three areas—growing as a believer, telling others about Christ, and glorifying Christ—has someone reading a prayer describing that area.

Before group members leave, encourage them to complete Week Fourteen in time for your next meeting.

WEEK 14 Unwrapping Your Gift

The Gifts of the Spirit

Overview

• to help group members understand the gifts of the Spirit.

• to give group members steps to discovering their own spiritual gift(s).

Scripture: I Corinthians 12:6-11, 28-30; Romans 12:6-8; Ephesians 4:11; I Peter 4:11

1 Getting Started

Housekeeping

Take some time to discuss with group members what everyone wants to do for the last meeting. Do some people want a week off before the final meeting? Do they want to plan some type of party for the final week? Make plans accordingly, and also decide what everyone wants to do regarding the next group study. Another study in the discipleship series is *No Turning Back*, which is about following Jesus.

Icebreaking

Tell your group members that since this week's study session is on spiritual gifts, you're going to send them on a little "scavenger hunt" to find theirs.

Before the meeting you will need to have gotten several Bibles, put them in boxes, and wrap them as gifts, complete with wrapping paper, ribbon—the whole works. Have enough so every group member will have a gift. Make a little card to put on the gift that reads, "To: (group member's name) From: God".

Before your meeting time, hide these somewhere either in your meeting area or outside (try to hide them extremely well). Tell group members that each of them has a spiritual gift hidden around the meeting area.

Explain to people that their gift will have their name on it. But instruct them not to open it, instead returning to where the group meets together. Award some sort of prize to the person who finds his or her "spiritual gift" and returns to the meeting spot the quickest.

When all the group members have found their gifts and have gathered back together, tell them that when the Bible study is over, they can open their gifts together.

Opening

Entering into this week's study time, you should try to be fostering a spirit of seeking after God as you try to ascertain what spiritual gifts God gave to you as a Christian.

A song that might help foster that mood is the song, "Seekers of Your Heart." Singing the following chorus a cappella is a great way to focus on God as you try to determine the gifts He's bestowed on your lives.

"Lord, we want to know You, lift our hearts to show You, all our love we owe You, we're seekers of Your heart."

Have group members pray silently to the Lord, asking Him to guide their efforts in determining what spiritual gift(s) they might have.

2 Bible Study

Focus

Have a group member read the story "What a Tour!" in Section I on page 125 of the journal. Once it's been read, ask: **Have you ever wondered, like John, whether or not you had a spiritual gift? What made you question if you had one?**

Let group members offer any thoughts and feelings they have. Ask them what they think of when they hear the term, "spiritual gift." Do they think people's talents and abilities fall under the category of spiritual gifts?

You may want to discuss a few of the questions located at the end of Section I. Mention the following scenario to group members, and tell them to think about it as you will be discussing it a little more later in the session.

John, the piano player on the youth tour, was told he has the spiritual gift of music. But John has a younger brother, Cody, who also plays the piano, and is the keyboard player for one of the top secular bands in the country. But Cody's group just had its latest album banned from stores due to its explicit lyrics.

Both John and Cody play the piano exceptionally well. Is John's piano playing a spiritual gift, like the elderly woman told him? And if so, what about Cody's? Would his piano playing be a spiritual gift, even though he apparently isn't using it for God's glory?

Dig In

Discuss the answer group members came up with for question one of Section II.

1. According to I Corinthians 12:8-11, where do spiritual gifts come from?

INSIDE INSIGHTS

■ The gift of speaking in tongues is most widely recognized two places in the Bible—being spoken of on the Day of Pentecost in Acts chapter 2, and being exercised by the Corinthian church in I Corinthians chapters 12–14. Some hold that the experience in I Corinthians means that the exercise of this gift in the church required that someone with the gift of interpretation "translate" the message to those who didn't understand the language. Others hold that because there was need of someone to interpret, this meant that the gift was something other than a foreign language.

■ One needs to look no farther than the Bible itself to find the discrediting of absolute, comprehensive "faith healing" for everyone. Some of the greatest men of faith during apostolic times suffered disease and sickness that even their great faith could not heal. Timothy had a stomach ailment (I Timothy 5:23), Epaphroditus was seriously ill (Philippians 2:30), and of course, Paul had his constant "thorn in the flesh" (II Corinthians 12:7-9). Though Paul had healed others (Acts 28:8), he left Trophimus unhealed (II Timothy 4:20). Of course, God is the author of all true healing.

Ask: **So if spiritual gifts come from the Holy Spirit, as the verses just indicated, where do spiritual gifts *not* come from?** Let group members respond with their ideas. If no one mentions them, explain that these gifts don't ultimately come from one's talents, natural gifts, or personality (although God may re-channel someone's inborn or learned ability for His usage). Then ask to see what people answered for question two of Section II.

2. Who receives these spiritual gifts (I Corinthians 12:7; see also Ephesians 4:7)?

The fact that Christians—as in *every Christian*—are the ones who receive spiritual gifts, bring up the story of John and Cody again, and ask: **After what we've just discussed in questions one and two, how would you answer the questions of whether or not John's piano playing was a spiritual gift, or if Cody's was also?**

See how group members respond, and use the following information as a guide: Neither brother's piano playing itself is a spiritual gift listed in the New Testament. But John's talent and ability may have been re-channeled for God's use, so it may have been the means used to "fuel" a spiritual gift, perhaps one of encouragement (Romans 12:8) as the elderly woman was encouraged by his playing.

Have group members describe in their own words the answers they came up with for question four of Section II.

After they've responded, say: **If the purpose of spiritual gifts is to build up (edify) other Christians, what are some ways we as Christians tear each other down, instead of edifying?**

Some possibilities could be slander (gossiping), envy, rage, accusing instead of forgiving and restoring when another Christian has fallen in sin, etc.

Now tell your group that you've seen where spiritual gifts come from, and what their purpose should be, but that there's still one glaring question: What *are* the gifts?

Say: **People communicate through body language, as well as verbal and nonverbal communication. When Christians use their spiritual gifts to build up other Christians, they're using Christianized body language. Maybe it's through a kind word, or maybe it's through some act of service, or just using their gifts in ways that show others that they are loved.**

Before you get into the meat of the session, have group members participate in a "body language" activity. Actually this is a glorified form of "charades."

On slips of paper, write down several specific scenarios for people to act out through body language. A few examples could be a bird pulling a worm out of the ground, a person catching a foul ball at a baseball game, a person taking off in an airplane for the first time, etc.

Put the slips of paper in a hat, and have group members randomly draw slips of paper out of the hat. Don't let group members say anything when they're using body language. Have other group members try to guess what scenario the person is depicting through his or her body language.

Have five group members read the five different passages listed in Section III. Then ask group members to read off the list of gifts they wrote down for each passage. When finished, divide group members into three subgroups, and have each subgroup take one of the three major categories of gifts listed in Section III.

Let each subgroup talk about the gifts in its category for a few minutes. Then meet back together as a whole group and let each subgroup tell the other subgroups what they talked about.

104

When all the gifts have been discussed, ask group members if they think a lot of the "spectacular gifts" happen in today's society. See how group members respond.

Ask: **With all the healers and miracle workers you see on television today, is there anything about them that might bother you or be unsettling? Explain.**

Let people respond who want to share. Explain that while things like healing and miracles indeed can still happen today, God does these things in response to prayer and His perfect will, not simply whenever someone claims to have power to make them happen at any time. All gifts call for testing (I Corinthians 14:29; I Thessalonians 5:21).

Leader's Tip: The area of spectacular gifts is an area that is extremely sensitive. Be careful not to advocate one position over another based on your personal feelings about it, because other group members may have come from backgrounds different from your experience. Instead, pray that whatever gifts Christians are given would be used for God's glory.

From the "Keep In Mind" section, go over the six ideas given to help discover what spiritual gift(s) they might have. Spend this time together as a group, so that people can feed off of the insights of others as well.

Reflect and Respond

Have group members reflect on what spiritual gifts they circled as thinking they might have (number one in Section III). Afterward, have group members look at the list of spiritual gifts in their journals. Then have them read the sections of Desire, Ability, Confirmation, and Blessing in the "Keep In Mind" section on pages 132-133 of the journal.

Challenge them in the coming week to try to answer those questions about any of the gifts (but especially the one(s) they circled). This may involve asking some Christian friends, as well as definitely asking themselves the questions in those sections.

Ask group members if any of them wrote down anything for question two of Section III. Ask them if they would be willing to share their comments with the rest of the group.

3 Sharing and Prayer

If your group members are feeling a little lost about what their spiritual gift(s) might be, brainstorm together to come up with a list of ideas or activities they could get involved in that might help them find out where their gift lies.

A few examples of things to try out could be:

• teaching younger kids

• volunteering for service in some area of the church or other Christian ministry

• getting involved in a Christian club on campus

• helping out someone who's already serving in a particular area of interest to you

• visiting a rescue mission, a home for the elderly, or an orphanage to see how you could help out.

Tell group members that *now* they can open the gifts they found at the start of the meeting time. Encourage them to use their gifts (the Bibles—in case you've forgotten what you wrapped up for them) to discover their spiritual gifts, and encourage them to keep seeking God and keep serving Him.

Close in prayer, asking God for the wisdom in the searching process for your spiritual gifts. Then get everyone together for a quick cheer celebrating next week—the last week of the book! Amen!

Oh yeah, before group members leave, encourage them to complete Week Fifteen in time for your next meeting (is there a pattern here?).

WEEK 15 Apples, Oranges, and Disciples

The Fruit of the Spirit

Overview

• to help group members better understand what the fruit of the Spirit is.

• to spiritually "pump up" group members by letting them know how they can be like Jesus by bearing that fruit in their own lives.

Scripture: John 15:4-8; Galatians 5:22-25; other selected passages regarding the fruit of the Spirit.

1 Getting Started

Housekeeping

By this point, your group members should know God like the back of their hands (well, maybe not quite that much!). Seriously, you should feel proud for having led the others through this 15-week study.

Spend some time having group members willingly discuss what the series has done in their spiritual lives, and how they believe they've come to know God a little bit better. Close this brief sharing time by telling the others how this time has impacted you, and what you hope it can do for all of your personal relationships with Christ.

Figure out what the group wants to do regarding the next study. If you're having a type of party or celebration to give the series a sense of closure, make any of those announcements (regarding food, music, etc.) before getting into your final study time.

Icebreaking

Since everyone will probably be pretty rowdy at this point, don't try to control their rowdiness! Instead, let it run wild (and hopefully, burn itself out!).

Explain that since this week's session is the *final* session, and that it's talking about the *fruit* of the Spirit, you've decided on an activity that involves both— sort of.

In your meeting place, mark off a square playing area big enough so that all the group members can be standing in the square together, but small enough that everyone can't be spread out too much.

Here's the plan: Hand everyone three or four balloons—like a red one, a yellow one, a green one, and an orange one. Tell everyone to blow up one of the colored balloons, but make sure everyone blows up the *same* color! Have them tie their balloons in a knot.

You need to bring a shoestring for every group member. Have group members tie their balloons around one of their ankles. Here's how the game is played.

Everyone has to stand in the square space with the balloons tied to their ankles. When you say, "Go," everyone tries to step on (and pop) everyone else's balloon, while preventing his or her own from being popped. The final person with an unpopped balloon will be the winner for that fruit category.

For example, let the red balloon signify an apple. Have the yellow balloon signify a banana, the green balloon—a kiwi, and the orange balloon—an orange.

Give each round's winner a piece of the actual fruit that his or her colored balloon represented.

Opening

It's probably a fairly safe bet that the group is still a bit rowdy. If so, a good rowdy praise song would be the old favorite, "Down in My Heart."

To refresh your memory, the song goes, "I've got the joy, joy, joy, joy, down in my heart, down in my heart, down in . . ."—you get the picture.

A few other aspects of the fruit of the Spirit (other than joy) that are incorporated into the song are, "I've got the love of Jesus, love of Jesus, down in my heart . . ." as well as "I've got the peace that passes understanding down in my heart. . . ."

If everyone's still into it, your group members may even want to try to make up some verses themselves that incorporate the other aspects of the fruit of the Spirit into the song.

When you're finished, pray to the Lord, asking that your study time will be "fruitful," in that group members can walk away confident that the Holy Spirit can help produce the fruit of the Spirit in their own lives.

2 Bible Study

Focus

Have one of your group members read the opening section "Don't Let Discouragement Get You Down" on page 135 of the journal.

When that's finished, ask group members which one of the examples struck them as the most amazing "overcoming obstacles" type of story. Make sure they explain their reasoning as to why they feel more strongly about one of the examples than the other.

Ask: **How did you feel about the description of the Christian?**

Do you tend to think of yourself more as someone who lets the Lord down

INSIDE
INSIGHTS

■ In Galatians 5:22, Paul refers to these nine character qualities as the "fruit of the Spirit." Uh, Paul, did you not take Grammar 101? Nine of something makes that something plural, so shouldn't it be the "fruits" of the Spirit instead? Actually, Paul purposely refers to them as fruit, because when you get the Spirit, you get the source of all fruit. So instead of thinking of this fruit as several different fruits—like apples, bananas, and oranges—think of them as the same kind of fruit, like a cluster of grapes.

■ Ever wonder why Paul, after listing the fruit of the Spirit in Galatians 5:22, 23, throws in the phrase, "against such things there is no law"? What does he mean? Actually, this phrase typifies Paul's whole reason for writing to the church of Galatia, because the church was falling away from it's freedom in Christ and back into Jewish "legalism." Things like circumcision and Jewish food laws were on the verge of being observed again. But Paul emphatically states, "against such things there is no law." And in I Timothy 1:8, 9, we read that although Paul thinks the law is good when used properly, he doesn't think it's for producing righteousness, as he goes on to list who the law is for in verses 9 and 10.

as a Christian, or more as someone who can produce spiritual character and be like Jesus with God's help? Explain.

Once any group members who are willing to share have done so, explain that this last session was designed to help them understand the various aspects of the fruit of the Spirit and how they can see those grow and help them "overcome obstacles" in their own Christian lives.

Leader's Tip: Be careful not to make group members feel guilty for not having more fruit of the Spirit evidenced in their lives than they do. Do this by encouraging them that developing those aspects of fruit in their lives is a process that will only develop if they walk in the Spirit.

 Dig In

 Ask group members to call out the answers they came up with for question one of Section II, "God's Produce Section." The answers are the fruit of *praise, good works, new Christians,* and *the spirit,* respectively.

Discuss the answers group members came up with for questions two and three of Section II.

2. According to John 15:2, 5, what can you discover about God's will for you in this area of bearing fruit?

3. What will be the result (John 15:8)?

After group members have shared their answers, comment: **We've read about the people that do bear more fruit and glorify God through their fruitfulness. But what does John 15:5, 6 say concerning those who don't bear fruit, thus not glorifying God?**

The Bible makes it clear that humans cannot be saved by any good works (or "acts of fruitfulness") in Ephesians 2:8, 9. But the Bible also makes it very clear that everyone who is saved will produce good works (Ephesians 2:10). Ask: **Have you ever heard a person described as someone who "says one thing, but does another"?** Let group members comment, and then explain that this is the point of James 2:14-26. Just as a stream cannot be both saltwater and freshwater, neither can a Christian be someone who claims to be one thing, while his or her life evidences something totally opposite.

Regardless, the main point to get across is the fact that good works should be naturally done as a *result* of being saved, not *in order* to be saved.

Divide your group members into three subgroups. Have one subgroup discuss the answers they came up with for the first three forms of the fruit of the Spirit in Section III. Have the second subgroup discuss their answers for the next three forms of the fruit of the Spirit described in Section IV, and have the third group discuss its answers for the last three forms of the fruit of the Spirit described in Section V.

After several minutes, have group members meet back together and discuss their answers and comments with the rest of the group.

Give everyone a chance to share his or her own answers with the whole group regarding the more personal questions. These questions would include questions five, six, seven, and ten in Section III; questions one, two, and five in Section IV; and questions one, four, five, six, and seven in Section V.

Ask: **When you read about the fruit of the Spirit, what are some areas you feel are not really evident in your life?** Have group members think to themselves about this. Then ask: **What do you think are some things you can do to develop more "fruit" in your life?** TRICK QUESTION!

Explain to group members that the only thing they are mandated to do is to "live by the Spirit" (Galatians 5:16) and let God take care of the rest. If aspects of the fruit of the Spirit aren't developing in their lives, then they need to evaluate whether or not they're totally living by the Spirit.

Reflect and Respond

Ask group members the following questions and spend some time by letting them discuss any answers or comments they might be willing to share:

• Am I totally "living by the Spirit" so that I'm open to God's developing aspects of the Spirit's fruit in my life?

• What are some areas or things in my life that might be hindering me from completely "living by the Spirit"?

Say: **Growth and development take time! If we just obey God and be open to following Him, He'll develop our fruit for us.**

3 Sharing and Prayer

Spend a few minutes together by making the following statement and opening it up for discussion. **How does it feel to know that we aren't required to do anything more than to "live by the Spirit" so God can develop righteousness in our lives?**

Let group members respond with their thoughts. When finished, tell everyone you enjoyed and were blessed by (hopefully you were) serving as the leader.

Encourage people to mention the one thing they've gotten out of this series, and how it's affected their spiritual lives. When finished, close with a time of prayer. Thank God for all of your group members by name, and requesting God that they would better live by the Spirit so forms of the fruit of the Spirit would develop in their lives.

Praise God that due to His love as the Father, the redemptive cross of Jesus the Son, and the personal ministry of the Holy Spirit, you will be *Never the Same!*